HTML5

Pocket Primer

HTML5
Pocket Primer

Oswald Campesato

MERCURY LEARNING AND INFORMATION
Dulles, Virginia
Boston, Massachusetts
New Delhi

Publisher: David Pallai
MERCURY LEARNING AND INFORMATION
22841 Quicksilver Drive
Dulles, VA 20166
info@merclearning.com
www.merclearning.com
1-800-758-3756

O. Campesato. *HTML5 Pocket Primer.*
ISBN: 978-1-938549-10-6

The publisher recognizes and respects all marks used by companies, manufacturers, and developers as a means to distinguish their products. All brand names and product names mentioned in this book are trademarks or service marks of their respective companies. Any omission or misuse (of any kind) of service marks or trademarks, etc. is not an attempt to infringe on the property of others.

Library of Congress Control Number: 2013942930

131415321   Printed in the United States of America
This book is printed on acid-free paper.

Our titles are available for adoption, license, or bulk purchase by institutions, corporations, etc.

For additional information, please contact the Customer Service Dept. at 1-800-758-3756 (toll free).
Digital versions of our titles are available at: www.authorcloudware.com

I'd like to dedicate this book to my parents –
may this bring joy and happiness into their lives.

PREFACE

WHAT YOU NEED TO KNOW FOR THIS BOOK

You need an understanding of CSS2 and a basic knowledge of HTML Web pages and JavaScript. If you want to be sure that you are able to absorb the material in this book, glance through some of the code samples to get an idea of how much is familiar to you and how much is new for you.

THE TARGET AUDIENCE

This book is intended to reach an international audience of readers with highly diverse backgrounds in various age groups. While many readers know how to read English, their native spoken language is not English (which could be their second, third, or even fourth language). Consequently, this book uses standard English rather than colloquial expressions that might be confusing to those readers. As you know, many people learn by different types of mimicry, which includes reading, writing, or hearing new material (yes, some basic videos are also available). This book takes these points into consideration in order to provide a comfortable and meaningful learning experience for the intended readers.

GETTING THE MOST FROM THIS BOOK

Some programmers learn well from prose, others learn well from sample code (and lots of it), which means that there's no single style that works perfectly for everyone.

Moreover, some programmers want to run the code first, see what it does, and then return to the code to understand the details (and others use the opposite approach).

Consequently, there is a variety of code samples in this book. Some are short, some are long, and other code samples "build" from earlier code samples.

The goal is to show (and not just tell) you a variety of visual effects that are possible, some of which you might not find anywhere else. You benefit from this approach because you can pick and choose the visual effects and the code that creates those visual effects.

WHY SO MANY CODE SAMPLES?

One of the primary rules of exposition of virtually any kind is "show, don't tell." Although that's not taken literally in this book, this is the motivation for showing first and telling second.

Perform a simple experiment: when you see the code samples and the accompanying graphics effects in this book, determine if it's more effective to explain ("tell") the visual effects or to show them.

If the adage "a picture is worth a thousand words" is true, then this book endeavors to provide both the pictures and the words.

DOESN'T THE DVD OBVIATE THE NEED FOR THIS BOOK?

The DVD contains all the code samples to save you time and effort from the error-prone process of manually typing code into an HTML Web page. In addition, there are situations in which you might not have easy access to DVD. Furthermore, the code samples in the book provide explanations that are not available on the DVD.

Finally, as mentioned earlier in this Preface, there are some introductory videos available that cover HTML5, CSS3, HTML5 Canvas, and SVG. Navigate to the publisher's Web site to obtain more information regarding their availability.

ACKNOWLEDGMENTS

Thanks to my lifelong friends Laurie Dresser and Farid Sharifi, and right now I cannot imagine anywhere else in the world that I would rather live than here in Silicon Valley.

I would be remiss if I did not thank Dave Pallai (publisher), Richard Clark (technical reviewer), and Rachel Leach (copy editor), who made valuable contributions to improve the quality of this book. As always, I take responsibility for any errors or omissions that you might find in any of the chapters.

ABOUT THE TECHNICAL EDITOR

Richard Clark, M.A. (@rdclark) is an experienced software developer and instructor for Kaazing Corporation. He has taught for Apple and Hewlett-Packard, written immersive simulations, developed multiple high-performance Web applications for the Fortune 100, and published Apple iOS applications. An in-demand speaker for international conferences, he has a special interest in using mobile, connected, real-time applications to help people live, work, and play better. In his spare time, Richard does Web development for non-profits, tends a garden full of California native plants, and cooks for family and charity events.

TABLE OF CONTENTS

CHAPTER 1

HTML5 SEMANTIC MARKUP

In this chapter, you will learn about the W3C and the WHATWG, and also about HTML5-specific elements for semantic markup. You will also learn about some Web sites that provide very useful information, such as browser support for HTML5 features. If you are new to HTML5, keep in mind that some of its features can vary considerably in terms of the complexity of their associated APIs. Fortunately, you can find jQuery plugins (and other tools) that provide a layer of abstraction over some of the more complex HTML5 APIs. Consequently, it's to your advantage to be aware of tools that can simplify your HTML5-related development.

WHAT IS HTML5?

HTML5 currently consists of a mixture of technologies, some of which are formally included in the HTML5 specification, and some which are not part of the specification. There are few people who seem to know the "definition" of HTML5, and perhaps that's why Peter Paul Koch (creator of the quirksmode Web site) wryly suggested that "whatever Web technology you're working on that's cool right now…that's HTML5." As you will discover, HTML5 means different things to different people, so don't be surprised if you cannot get one consistent "definition" of HTML5 (if only the situation were so simple!).

HTML5 is the latest version of HTML that is designed with a plugin-free architecture that is backward compatible with most features of earlier versions of HTML markup. HTML5 provides a wealth of new features: new tags for audio, video, semantic markup; new input types and validation for forms; local and session storage; support for graphics-based APIs in Canvas; and server-sent events and WebSockets.

Although CSS3 is not a formal part of HTML5, many people consider it to be an important part of HTML5 Web pages. As you will see in Chapters 2 and

3, CSS3 provides support for rich visual effects; in Chapter 4, you will learn about some of the powerful new functionality in CSS3 (such as CSS Shaders).

You have probably seen many Web pages with HTML markup that relies on a combination of HTML <table> elements and HTML <div> elements. Such tags are generic, and it can be difficult to determine what role each one plays in the finished page. The good news is that the new HTML5 semantic tags provide more meaningful information about the purpose of each section in an HTML5 Web page, which can be discerned much more easily than Web pages written in HTML4. You will see an example of using some of these semantic tags later in this chapter.

One of the exciting aspects of HTML5 is that it's designed to run on desktop devices as well as mobile devices. In fact, HTML5-based mobile applications offer speed of development and deployment to multiple mobile devices with one code base, which is appealing to developers of mobile applications that do not require intensive computations (such as games) or access to hardware features (such as accelerometers).

Keep in mind that support for native application features (such as offline mode, location lookup, file system access, and camera) in modern browsers on the mobile platform often lags behind the corresponding support for desktop releases. In addition, Web-based mobile applications do not support several Android-specific features, such as adding ringtones, performing notifications, or changing the wallpaper. However, you can transfer files using the regular AJAX API (XmlHTTPRequest), and file APIs are supported on Android (via JavaScript), with upcoming iOS support:

http://caniuse.com/#feat=fileapi

There is one other point to keep in mind: the specification for HTML 4.01 was introduced in 1999, so HTML5 represents the largest advance in HTML in ten years, and perhaps the inclusion of other technologies was inevitable. There is a great deal of excitement surrounding HTML5, and a major update regarding the specification is scheduled for 2014. Indeed, the enthusiasm for HTML5 may have accelerated the speed with which HTML5 will become a formal specification based on open standards.

BROWSER SUPPORT FOR HTML5

The WebKit-based browsers (Chrome and Safari), Mozilla Firefox, Opera, and IE10 support many HTML5 features, on desktops as well as mobile devices. The Dolphin browser and the browser provided by the Tizen OS were the top-ranked browsers in terms of support for HTML5 features in 2012.

As you know, this book focuses on WebKit-based browsers, and all code samples have been tested on a Chrome browser on a Macbook. In addition, virtually every code sample in this book can be deployed on at least one of the following devices:

• An Asus Prime™ tablet with Android ICS (Ice Cream Sandwich)

- A Nexus 7™ with Android JB (JellyBean)
- An iPad™ running on iOS 5 or later
- A Sprint Nexus™ S 4G with Android ICS (or higher)

The only exceptions are the code samples (and associated screenshots) in Chapter 4 that illustrate the most recent features of CSS3 (such as CSS Shaders) that are rendered in a special Chromium build from Adobe that is installed on a Macbook. The download link for this special build is in Chapter 3, and you can expect these new CSS3 features to be supported in the near future. In fact, work is already underway on CSS Blending and Compositing:

http://www.webkit.org/blog/2102/last-week-in-webkit-a-new-content-security-policy-api-and-transitioning-from-percentages-to-pixels

HTML5 AND VARIOUS WORKING GROUPS

The *W3C* (World Wide Web Consortium), the *WHATWG* (Web Hypertext Application Technology Working Group), and the *DAP* (Device APIs Working Group) are organizations that provide the specifications and APIs for HTML5 and mobile devices that are covered in this book. In addition, the IETF (Internet Engineering Task Force) handles the networking standards (such as WebSockets, SPDY, CORS, and so forth), but not the actual APIs. Its homepage is here:

https://www.ietf.org/

The W3C is an international community for various groups to work together in order to develop web standards. The W3C is led by Web inventor Tim Berners-Lee and CEO Jeffrey Jaffe. Its homepage is here:

http://www.w3.org

Every proposal submitted to the W3C undergoes the following sequence in order to become a W3C Recommendation:

- Working Draft (WD)
- Candidate Recommendation (CR)
- Proposed Recommendation (PR)
- W3C Recommendation (REC)
- Later revisions

The HTML5-related technologies that have been submitted to the W3C are in different stages of the W3C "evaluation" process. The following link contains a diagram that provides a succinct visual display of HTML5 technologies and their status in December, 2011:

http://en.wikipedia.org/wiki/File:HTML5-APIs-and-related-technologies-by-Sergey-Mavrody.png

If you want to find the most recent status updates, the following link provides a list of HTML5 APIs and their status:

http://www.w3.org/TR/

Click on the link "JavaScript APIs" in the preceding Web site, or simply navigate to this URL, which shows you the most recent status of HTML5 APIs:

http://www.w3.org/TR/#tr_Javascript_APIs

The WHATWG focuses primarily on the development of HTML and APIs needed for Web applications. The WHATWG was founded in 2004 by employees of Apple, the Mozilla Foundation, and Opera Software. The main focus of the WHATWG is the HTML standard, which also includes Web Workers, Web Storage, the WebSockets API, and server-sent events. Two links with additional information about the WHATWG:

http://www.whatwg.org/
http://wiki.whatwg.org/wiki/FAQ

HTML5 is a joint effort involving the W3C and the WHATWG. If you enjoy reading proposals, you will find links for various W3C Specifications, mainly in this chapter and Chapter 10.

Another group is the Device APIs Working Group, whose mission is to create client-side APIs that enable the development of web applications and Web widgets that interact with devices services such as calendar, contacts, camera, and so forth. Currently the DAP is actively working on the following specifications:

- Battery Status API
- HTML Media Capture
- Media Capture and Streams (access to `getUserMedia`)
- Network Information API
- Proximity Events
- Vibration API
- Web Intents (service discovery)

Additional information about the status of these (and other) DAP specifications is here:

http://www.w3.org/2009/dap/

HTML5 SPECIFICATIONS: W3C OR WHATWG?

In essence, the WHATWG has the master specification, which the W3C HTML Working Group takes as the foundation for the "official" specification. The W3C synchronizes its work with the WHATWG, mostly reformatting to match its publication style (including breaking it into sub-specifications.)

The exact list of changes in the introduction to the WHATWG form of the specification is here:

*http://www.whatwg.org/specs/web-apps/current-work/multipage/
introduction.html#introduction*

Now that you know a little bit about the groups that are in charge of various specifications, let's explore some of the facets of HTML5, which is the subject of the next section.

WHAT TECHNOLOGIES ARE INCLUDED IN HTML5?

The following list contains a combination of technologies are formally included in the HTML5 specification, as well as several other technologies that are frequently associated with HTML5:

- Canvas 2D
- CSS3
- Drag and Drop (DnD)
- File API
- Geolocation
- Microdata
- Offline Applications
- Server-Sent Events (SSE)
- SVG
- Web Intents
- Web Messaging
- Web Storage
- WebSockets
- Web Workers

There are other technologies that are often associated with HTML5, including WebGL and XHR2 (XmlHTTPRequest Level 2).

Incidentally, the following link contains a diagram that provides a succinct visual display of HTML5 technologies and their status in December 2011:

*http://en.wikipedia.org/wiki/File:HTML5-APIs-and-related-technologies-
by-Sergey-Mavrody.png*

The preceding link classifies HTML5 technologies as follows:

- W3C Recommendation
- Candidate Recommendation
- Last Call
- Working Draft
- Non-W3C Specification
- Deprecated W3C APIs

Keep in mind that the status of some of these technologies will change, so be sure to visit the link with the details of the W3C specification for each in order to find their most recent status. In addition, many of the HTML5 technologies in the preceding diagram are covered in Chapter 10, often with jQuery plugins that provide a layer of abstraction over HTML5 technologies.

DIFFERENCES BETWEEN HTML4 TAGS AND HTML5 TAGS

Broadly speaking, HTML5 differs from earlier versions of HTML in the following ways:

- Some HTML4.x elements are no longer supported
- Supports new elements
- Simplifies some existing elements
- Supports custom attributes

Some new tags in HTML5 include: `<article>`, `<aside>`, `<audio>`, `<canvas>`, `<command>`, `<datalist>`, `<details>`, `<dialog>`, `<figure>`, `<footer>`, `<header>`, `<hgroup>`, `<keygen>`, `<mark>`, `<meter>`, `<nav>`, `<output>`, `<progress>`, `<rp>`, `<rt>`, `<ruby>`, `<section>`, `<source>`, `<time>`, and `<video>`.

The HTML elements that are not recommended for new work in HTML5 (many of which have been replaced with CSS styling) include the following: `<acronym>`, `<applet>`, `<basefont>`, `<big>`, `<center>`, `<dir>`, `<font>`, `<frame>`, `<frameset>`, `<noframes>`, `<s>`, `<strike>`, `<tt>`, and `<u>`.

You are probably already aware of the new HTML5 `<audio>` tag and HTML5 `<video>` tag. Later in this chapter, you'll see examples of how to use these tags in HTML5 Web pages.

One underrated new HTML5 feature is support for custom data attributes, which always have a `data-` prefix. This support for custom data attributes provides HTML5 markup with some of the functionality that is available in XML, which enables code to process custom tags and their values and also pass validation at the same time. In fact, jQuery Mobile makes *very* extensive use of custom data attributes, as you will see in an example later in this chapter.

If you want additional details, you'll find a full list of the differences between HTML5 and HTML4 in this W3C document:

http://dev.w3.org/html5/html4-differences/

USEFUL ONLINE TOOLS FOR HTML5 DEVELOPMENT

Before delving into the new HTML5 tags that are discussed in this chapter, you need to know about the online tools that can assist in creating well-designed HTML5 Web pages. These tools are available because of one important fact: modern browsers differ in terms of their support for HTML5 features (for desktop browsers and also for mobile browsers). Fortunately, tools such as Modernizr enable you to detect HTML5 feature support in modern browsers using simple JavaScript code.

Modernizr

Modernizr is a very useful tool for HTML5-related feature detection in various browsers. Its homepage is here:

http://www.modernizr.com/

Server-side "browser sniffing" used to be a popular technique for detecting the browser that you were using to render a particular Web page, but this technique is no longer as accurate (or as "clean") due to rapidly changing implementations in browsers. Indeed, the most popular Web sites that check for HTML5 support use feature detection and not browser sniffing.

At some point you will start using JavaScript in your HTML5 Web pages (indeed, you probably do so already). Modernizr provides a programmatic way to check for many HTML5 and CSS3 features in different browsers.

In order to use Modernizr, include the following code snippet in the `<head>` element of your Web pages:

```
<script src="modernizr.min.js" type="text/ javascript"> </script>
```

The following type of code block illustrates one way that you can use Modernizr in an HTML page:

```
if(Modernizr.canvas) {
    // canvas is available
    // do something here
} else {
    // canvas is not available
    // do something else here
}
```

Navigate to the Modernizr homepage where you can read the documentation, tutorials, and details regarding the set of feature detection.

Caniuse

The Caniuse Web site ("When Can I Use...") is extremely useful because it provides information regarding support for many HTML5 features in modern browsers:

http://www.caniuse.com

Currently there are two main tabs on this Web site. The first (and default) tab is divided into a number of sections (CSS, HTML5, SVG, JS API, and Other). Each section contains a list of technical items that are hyperlinks to other Web pages that provide detailed information.

The second tab on this Web site is called "tables." When you click on this tab you will see a tabular display of information in a set of tables. The columns in each table are modern browsers, the rows specify features, and the cells in the tables provide the browser version numbers where the specified features are supported.

In addition, the following Web sites also provide very useful information regarding HTML5:

http://mobilehtml5.org/
http://www.quirksmode.org/mobile/
http://html5boilerplate.com/

DESIGNING HTML5 WEB PAGES

There are two main perspectives from which to go about designing HTML5 Web pages: graceful degradation and progressive enhancement. Each perspective uses different approaches for Web page design, as discussed briefly in the following sub-sections. As for online tools, the Web site HTML5 BoilerPlate is a very useful tool for both approaches.

Graceful Degradation

This technique assumes that the functionality in a Web page is supported across multiple browsers; in situations where a feature is unavailable in a specific browser, a "fallback" message is sometimes provided. You undoubtedly have seen examples of this technique whereby HTML elements include the text string "this feature is not supported" when the HTML element is not supported. For example, the code samples in this book that contain HTML5 <canvas> elements will always provide such a fallback message.

According to the YUI Web site (*https://yuilibrary.com/yui/docs/tutorials/gbs/*), graceful degradation "prioritizes *presentation*, and permits less widely-used browsers to receive less (and give less to the user). Progressive enhancement puts *content* at the center, and allows most browsers to receive more (and show more to the user)."

Although this concept is hardly new (in fact, you can find links from 1998 that discuss graceful degradation), it seems to be experiencing a resurgence of interest recently.

Progressive Enhancement

This technique involves a sort of bottom-up approach: start with a core set of features that work across multiple browsers, and then gradually add new functionality. Progressive enhancement makes basic content of a particular Web page accessible to all users, and users who have better browsers will have access to an enhanced version of that Web page. Toolkits such as Modernizr allow you to use progressive enhancement. One point to keep in mind is that progressive enhancement can be more challenging for Web pages that make very heavy use of JavaScript for user interaction. Perform an Internet search to find online articles that provide additional information about progressive enhancement.

RESPONSIVE DESIGN

Responsive Web design refers to the concept of creating Web sites in such a way that the layout and the elements "adapt" to conform to the device on which the Web site is viewed. In simplified terms, responsive Web design involves the use of media queries, flexible layouts, and flexible images and media.

Ethan Marcotte wrote an excellent article about responsive Web design:

http://www.alistapart.com/articles/responsive-web-design/

A collection of fifteen articles that discuss responsive Web design is available here:

http://designwoop.com/2012/03/15-detailed-responsive-web-design-tutorials/

An Internet search will yield a number of additional articles regarding responsive Web design. You can also find numerous jQuery plugins for responsive Web design here:

http://designbeep.com/2012/03/28/38-useful-and-effective-jquery-plugins-for-responsive-web-design/

If you are unfamiliar with jQuery, then the plugins in the preceding link will make more sense after you have read the jQuery chapters in this book.

If you prefer to start with a template for responsive design instead of designing your own "from scratch," a template is available here:

http://verekia.com/initializr/responsive-template

Finally, a responsive design development kit is Skeleton, which is style agnostic and also designed to scale well among various devices. Its homepage is here:

http://getskeleton.com/

A SIMPLE HTML5 WEB PAGE

In addition to introducing many new semantic tags, HTML5 has simplified several tags, including the `<DOCTYPE>` declaration and the attributes `lang` and `charset`. Listing 1.1 displays `Sample1.html`, which is an HTML5 Web page that illustrates the simplified syntax of HTML5.

LISTING 1.1 Sample1.html

```
<!doctype html>
<html lang="en">
  <head>
   <meta charset="utf-8" />
   <title>This is HTML5</title>
  </head>

  <body>
   <div id="outer"></div>
```

```
<body>
</html>
```

Listing 1.1 contains an HTML5 `<!DOCTYPE>` element whose simple structure is very intuitive and easy to remember, especially in comparison to the syntax for an HTML4 `<!DOCTYPE>` element (try to construct one from memory!). This markup is backward-compatible: it triggers standards mode in all browsers that have standards mode (versus quirks mode) and it also tells the browser to use the special HTML5 parsing mode.

In addition, the `<meta>` tag and its attributes `lang` and `charset` attributes are simpler than their counterparts in earlier versions of HTML. Note that HTML5 supports the new syntax as well as the earlier syntax, so your existing HTML pages will be recognized in HTML5.

NEW HTML5 ELEMENTS

This section discusses some of the useful new elements in HTML5, which includes semantic-related elements, the `<video>` element, and the `<audio>` element. The new types for the `<input>` element are discussed in the section for HTML5 forms (later in this chapter). A modest knowledge of the new HTML5 tags is required in order to follow the examples in this book, so you can skim through this section if you do not require extensive knowledge of HTML5 elements.

Semantic Markup HTML5 Elements

HTML5 provides new elements for "semantic markup" that designed to provide more meaningful structure in your HTML5 Web pages. Some of these new tags are: `<section>`, `<article>`, `<aside>`, `<nav>`, `<header>`, `<hgroup>`, `<canvas>`, `<video>`, `<audio>`, `<time>`, `<figure>`, and `<figcaption>`.

For example, the HTML5 `<section>` tag can be used as a "container" for a document, whereas the HTML5 `<article>` tag is well-suited for representing the content of newspaper article or a blog post. The HTML5 `<header>` tag and HTML5 `<footer>` tag represent the header and footer of an HTML5 `<section>` tag. The HTML5 `<aside>` tag contains information that is somewhat related to the primary content of a Web page (similar in nature to a "by the way" type of comment).

The HTML5 `<nav>` tag supports navigation for a section of a document in a Web page. Other new tags include the HTML5 `<dialog>` tag for marking up conversations and the HTML5 `<figure>` tag for associating a caption for videos or graphics (which is useful for search engines).

The semantics of these tags are straightforward, yet there are some subtler aspects that you will learn as you gain experience with HTML5 Web pages.

Semantic markup also includes WAI-ARIA (Web Accessibility Initiative—Accessible Rich Internet Applications). In brief, WAI-ARIA is a "bridging" technology that clarifies semantics of assistive technologies. The WAI-ARIA specification describes the roles, states, and properties that define accessible user interface elements, which are described (along with `aria-*` attributes on HTML elements) here:

http://dev.w3.org/html5/spec/wai-aria.html

Article Versus Section: How Are They Used?

The following simple example illustrates the use of the words "article" and "section." A newspaper can contain multiple sections, and each section can contain multiple articles; furthermore, an article can contain multiple sections. Thus, a section contains articles that in turn contain sections, which is a `tag1-contains-tag2-contains-tag1` hierarchical scenario. Obviously this situation can make it more difficult to understand the intended usage of a `<section>` element and an `<article>` element in a length and complex HTML Web page that contains many of these elements.

The contents of an HTML5 `<article>` element are considered ready for syndication, whereas the contents of an HTML5 `<section>` element that is a child element of an HTML5 `<article>` element is somewhat comparable to a blog post (but keep in mind that a blog post can be an article, so this analogy is only partially valid). On the other hand, an HTML5 `<section>` element that contains one or more HTML5 `<article>` elements is considered "a thematic grouping of content."

However, you might encounter HTML5 Web pages containing semantic markup elements that are used incorrectly, or you might inadvertently create such pages during your own work. You can consider the possibility of inserting one or more `data-` attributes to provide more context-specific information intended purpose of deeply nested HTML elements (recall the days when you had to deal with HTML Web pages with "div forests").

Before you use the `<section>` and `<article>` elements for content in an HTML5 Web page, think of the logical relationship of the content in order to determine the structural layout of your HTML5 Web page. If there is any possibility for confusion, it might also be helpful to include a comment section to make it easier for other people to understand the rationale for the layout of your HTML5 Web page.

Why Use Semantic Markup?

There are at least two reasons for using semantic tags in your Web pages. First, semantic tags can help you understand the structure of a Web page and the purpose of a section of markup. Second, the use of semantic tags makes it easier for you to programmatically locate and manage sets of logically similar sections of code (such as `<nav>` elements, `<aside>` elements, and so forth). Third, screen-readers and search engines can use these tags to separate the content from navigation in a Web page. These are several of the more important reasons for using semantic markup, and you can probably think of other reasons as well.

Incidentally, jQuery Mobile uses custom attributes (which always start with the string "data-") as a way to embed data that can be accessed programmatically, and to a lesser extent, sort of "document" different sections of a Web page. Later in this section you will see an example of a jQuery Mobile Web page that uses custom attributes.

A Simple Web Page with Semantic Markup

Listing 1.2 displays the contents of SemanticMarkup1.html that illustrates how to use HTML5 semantic markup.

LISTING 1.2 SemanticMarkup1.html

```
<!DOCTYPE HTML>
<html>
<head>
   <meta charset="utf-8" />
   <title>Examples of HTML5 Semantic Markup </title>
 </head>

 <body>
  <article> <!-- start article #1 -->
    <header>
       <h1>An HTML5 CSS3 Canvas Graphics Primer</h1>
    </header>

    <header>
        <aside style="font-size:larger;font-style:italic;color:red;
float:right;width:150px;">
        The book is available on Amazon as well as MercLearning.
        </aside>
<p>This book covers the features of HTML5 Canvas graphics and CSS3
graphics, and shows how to extend the power of CSS3 with SVG.<p>
<p>The material is accessible to people with basic knowledge of
HTML and JavaScript, and more advanced users will benefit from the
examples of sophisticated CSS3 2D/3D animation effects.</p>
<p>Learn how to create HTML5 web pages that use Canvas, CSS3, and
SVG to render 2D shapes and Bezier curves, create linear and radial
gradients, apply transforms to 2D shapes and JPG files, create
animation effects, and generate 2D/3D bar charts and line graphs.<p>

        <nav>
        <ul>
            <li><a href="http://www.amazon.ca/HTML5-Canvas-CSS3-
Graphics-Primer/dp/1936420341">Amazon Link</a></li>
            <li><a href="http://www.merclearning.com/titles/html5_
canvas_css3_graphics.html
">MercLearning Link</a></li>
        </ul>
        </nav>

        <details>
        <summary>More Details About the Book</summary>
<p>The code samples in this book run on WebKit-based browsers on
desktops and tablets.  A companion DVD contains all the source code
and color graphics in the book.</p>
```

```
      </details>
    </header>

    <section>
      <h3>Other Books by the Author</h3>
      <article> <!-- start article #2 -->
        <p>Previous books include: Java Graphics Programming, Web
2.0 Fundamentals, SVG Fundamentals, and Pro Android Flash.<p>
        <footer>
          <p>Posted by: Oswald Campesato</p>
        </footer>
        <details>
        <summary>More Details</summary>
        <p>Contact me for more detailed information</p>
        </details>
      </article> <!-- end article #2 -->

      <article> <!-- start article #3 -->
<p>SVCC (Silicon Valley Code Camp) is the biggest free code camp in
the world, and also a great way to meet like-minded people who are
interested in the latest trends in technology.</p>
        <img src="ThreeSpheres1.png" width="200" height="100" />
      </article> <!-- end article #3 -->
    </section>
  </article> <!-- end article #1 -->
 </body>
</html>
```

The <body> tag in Listing 1.2 contains an HTML5 <article> tag that in turn contains two HTML5 <header> tags, where the second HTML5 <header> tag contains an HTML5 <aside>. The next part of Listing 1.2 contains an HTML5 <nav> element with three HTML <a> links for navigation.

Figure 1.1 displays the result of rendering the Web page Semantic-Markup1.html in a Chrome browser.

The HTML5 <hgroup> Element

The HTML5 <hgroup> element enables you to "group" together a set of heading-related tags inside an HTML5 <header> element. The HTML5 <hgroup> element must contain at least two of the <h1> through <h6> elements (and nothing else). The purpose of this element is similar to that of a nested outline: it is for grouping a title with one or more subtitles.

NOTE The HTML5 <hgroup> element can *only* contain <h1> through <h6> elements, whereas an HTML5 <header> element can contain <h1> through <h6> *as well as* other HTML elements. If you do not need an <hgroup> subtitle or other <header> content, simply use the <h1> through <h6> elements.

The indentation of the tags inside the HTML5 <hgroup> element is displayed in a "local" hierarchical fashion that is distinct from the normal hierarchical display of heading tags.

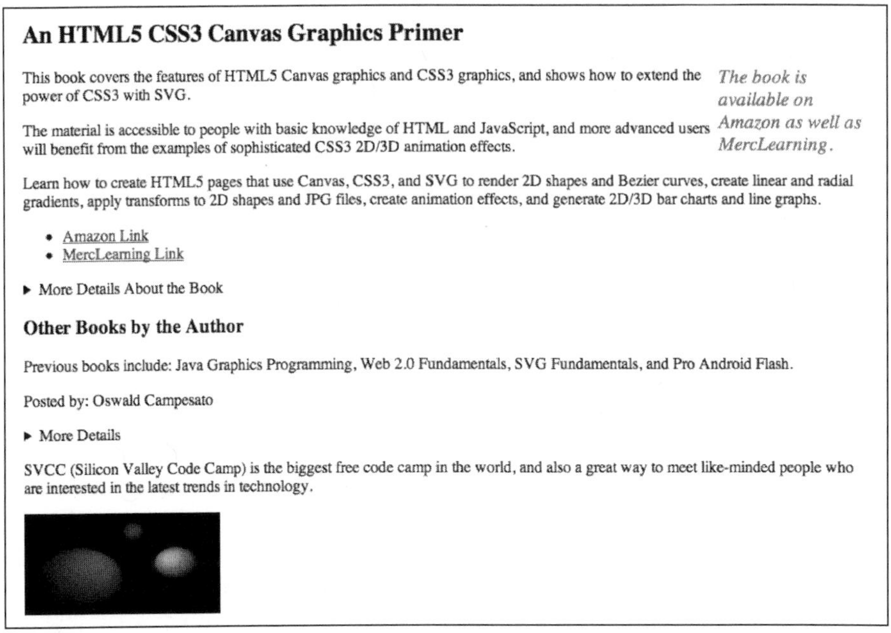

An HTML5 CSS3 Canvas Graphics Primer

This book covers the features of HTML5 Canvas graphics and CSS3 graphics, and shows how to extend the power of CSS3 with SVG.   *The book is available on Amazon as well as MercLearning.*

The material is accessible to people with basic knowledge of HTML and JavaScript, and more advanced users will benefit from the examples of sophisticated CSS3 2D/3D animation effects.

Learn how to create HTML5 pages that use Canvas, CSS3, and SVG to render 2D shapes and Bezier curves, create linear and radial gradients, apply transforms to 2D shapes and JPG files, create animation effects, and generate 2D/3D bar charts and line graphs.

- Amazon Link
- MercLearning Link

▸ More Details About the Book

Other Books by the Author

Previous books include: Java Graphics Programming, Web 2.0 Fundamentals, SVG Fundamentals, and Pro Android Flash.

Posted by: Oswald Campesato

▸ More Details

SVCC (Silicon Valley Code Camp) is the biggest free code camp in the world, and also a great way to meet like-minded people who are interested in the latest trends in technology.

FIGURE 1.1 An HTML5 Web page with semantic markup in a Chrome browser

The following simple code fragment shows you how to use an HTML5 `<hgroup>` element inside an HTML5 `<header>` element:

```
<header>
 <hgroup>
  <h1>Title of post One</h1>
  <h2>subtitle of the post One</h2>
 </hgroup>
 <p>posted 12-10-2012</p>
</header>
```

Although the HTML5 `<hgroup>` element can be useful, it is not a high-priority item in this chapter, so we will not provide a complete code sample. However, you can easily copy/paste the preceding code block into an HTML5 Web page and see the results when you launch the Web page in a browser.

Custom Data Attributes in HTML5

HTML5 supports custom data attributes, which effectively enables you to write HTML5 Web pages in which you can store custom data that is private to the Web page or application.

Listing 1.3 displays the contents of the Web page `CustomAtributes1.html` that illustrates some of the custom attributes that are available in jQuery Mobile.

LISTING 1.3 CustomAttributes1.html

```
<!doctype html>
<html lang="en">
  <head>
   <meta charset="utf-8" />
   <title>Hello World from jQueryMobile</title>
  </head>

  <body>
    <div id="page1" data-role="page">
      <header data-role="header" data-position="fixed">
        <h1>jQuery Mobile</h1>
      </header>

      <div class="content" data-role="content">
        <h3>Content Area</h3>
      </div>

      <footer data-role="footer" data-position="fixed">
        <h3>Fixed Footer</h3>
      </footer>
    </div>
  </body>
</html>
```

Listing 1.3 displays the structure of an HTML5 Web page for jQuery Mobile, but it is incomplete because it does not contain references to any jQuery JavaScript files or CSS stylesheets. The purpose of Listing 1.3 is to shows you the layout of a simple jQuery Mobile page, which in this case consists of one so-called "page view," along with some of the custom data attributes that are common in jQuery Mobile. We will delve into jQuery Mobile Web pages in greater detail in Chapters 8 and 9.

SUMMARY

This chapter provided an overview of several HTML5-related techniques for managing and persisting user-provided data using HTML5 Forms. In this chapter, you learned how to do the following:

- Create HTML5 Web pages
- Use new semantic markup
- Distinguish between <section> and <article> tags
- Use custom data attributes
- Use online tools for HTML5 development

INTRODUCTION TO CSS3

This chapter introduces various aspects of CSS3, such as 2D/3D graphics and 2D/3D animation. In some cases, CSS3 concepts are presented without code samples due to space limitations; however, those concepts are included because it's important for you to be aware of their existence. By necessity, this chapter assumes that you have a moderate understanding of CSS, which means that you know how to set properties in CSS selectors. If you are unfamiliar with CSS selectors, there are many introductory articles available through an Internet search. If you are convinced that CSS operates under confusing and seemingly arcane rules, then it's probably worth your while to read an online article about CSS box rules, after which you will have a better understanding of the underlying logic of CSS.

The first part of this chapter contains code samples that illustrate how to create shadow effects, how to render rectangles with rounded corners, and also how to use linear and radial gradients. The second part of this chapter covers CSS3 transforms (scale, rotate, skew, and translate), along with code samples that illustrate how to apply transforms to HTML elements and to JPG files.

The third part of this chapter covers CSS3 3D graphics and animation effects, and the fourth part of this chapter briefly discusses CSS3 media queries, which enable you to detect some characteristics of a device, and therefore render an HTML5 Web page based on those properties.

You can launch the code samples in this chapter in a `Webkit`-based browser on a desktop or a laptop; you can also view them on mobile devices, provided that you launch them in a browser that supports the CSS3 features that are used in the code samples. For your convenience, many of the code samples in this chapter are accompanied by screenshots of the code samples on a Sprint Nexus S 4G and an Asus Prime Android ICS 10" tablet (both on Android ICS), which enables you to compare those screenshots with the corresponding images that are rendered on `WebKit-based browser` on desktops and laptops. In

Chapter 9, you will learn the process of creating Android applications that can launch HTML5 Web pages. Don't forget that the Android `apk` files are available on the accompanying DVD, and you can launch them on an Android that supports Android ICS (or higher).

CSS3 SUPPORT AND BROWSER-SPECIFIC PREFIXES FOR CSS3 PROPERTIES

Before we delve into the details of CSS3, there are two important details that you need to know about defining CSS3-based selectors for HTML pages. First, you need to know the CSS3 features that are available in different browsers. One of the best Web sites for determining browser support for CSS3 features is here:

http://caniuse.com/

The preceding link contains tabular information regarding CSS3 support in IE, Firefox, Safari, Chrome, and Opera.

Another highly useful tool that checks for CSS3 feature support is `Enhance.js`, which tests browsers to determine whether or not they can support a set of essential CSS and JavaScript properties, and then delivering features to those browsers that satisfies the test. You can download `Enhance.js` here:

https://github.com/filamentgroup/EnhanceJS

The second detail that you need to know is that many CSS3 properties currently require browser-specific prefixes in order for them to work correctly. The prefix applies to "work in progress" for individual browsers, and the final specification drops browser-specific prefixes. The prefixes `-ie-`, `-moz-`, and `-o-` are for Internet Explorer, Firefox, and Opera, respectively. Note that Opera also supports `-webkit-` prefixes, and it's possible that other browsers will do the same (check the respective Web sites for updates).

As an illustration, the following code block shows examples of these prefixes:

```
-ie-webkit-border-radius: 8px;
-moz-webkit-border-radius: 8px;
-o-webkit-border-radius: 8px;
border-radius: 8px;
```

In your CSS selectors, specify the attributes with browser-specific prefixes before the "generic" attribute, which serves as a default choice in the event that the browser-specific attributes are not selected. The CSS3 code samples in this book contain `WebKit`-specific prefixes, which helps us keep the CSS stylesheets manageable in terms of size. If you need CSS stylesheets that work on multiple browsers (for current versions as well as older versions), there are essentially two options available. One option is to manually add the CSS3 code with all the required browser-specific prefixes, which can be tedious to maintain and error-prone. Another option is to use CSS toolkits or frameworks (discussed in the next chapter) that can programmatically generate the CSS3 code that contains all browser-specific prefixes.

Finally, an extensive list of browser-prefixed CSS properties is here:

http://peter.sh/experiments/vendor-prefixed-css-property-overview/

QUICK OVERVIEW OF CSS3 FEATURES

CSS3 adopts a modularized approach involving multiple sub-specifications for extending existing CSS2 functionality as well as supporting new functionality. As such, CSS3 can be logically divided into the following categories:

- Backgrounds/borders
- Color
- Media queries
- Multi-column layout
- Selectors

With CSS3 you can create boxes with rounded corners and shadow effects; create rich graphics effects using linear and radial gradients; detect portrait and landscape mode; detect the type of mobile device using media query selectors; and produce multi-column text rendering and formatting.

In addition, CSS3 enables you to define sophisticated node selection rules in selectors using pseudo-classes, first or last child (`:first-child`, `:last-child`, `:first-of-type`, and `:last-of-type`), and also pattern-matching tests for attributes of elements. Several sections in this chapter contain examples of how to create such selection rules.

CSS3 PSEUDO CLASSES AND ATTRIBUTE SELECTION

This brief section contains examples of some pseudo-classes, followed by snippets that show you how to select elements based on the relative position of text strings in various attributes of those elements. Although this section focuses on the `:nth-child()` pseudo-class, you will become familiar with various other CSS3 pseudo-classes and in the event that you need to use those pseudo-classes, a link is provided at the end of this section which contains more information and examples that illustrate how to use them.

CSS3 supports an extensive and rich set of pseudo-classes, including `nth-child()`, along with some of its semantically related "variants," such as `nth-of-type()`, `nth-first-of-type()`, `nth-last-of-type()`, and `nth-last-child()`.

CSS3 also supports Boolean selectors (which are also pseudo-classes) such as `empty`, `enabled`, `disabled`, and `checked`, which are very useful for Form-related HTML elements. One other pseudo class is `not()`, which returns a set of elements that do not match the selection criteria.

CSS3 uses the meta-characters ^, $, and * (followed by the = symbol) in order to match an initial, terminal, or arbitrary position for a text string. If you are familiar with the Unix utilities `grep` and `sed`, as well as the `vi` text editor, then these meta-characters are very familiar to you.

CSS3 Pseudo Classes

The CSS3 `:nth-child()` pseudo-class is both powerful and useful, and it has the following form:

```
:nth-child(insert-a-keyword-or-linear-expression-here)
```

The following list provides various examples of using the `nth-child()` pseudo-class in order to match various subsets of child elements of an HTML `<div>` element (which can be substituted by other HTML elements as well):

`div:nth-child(1)`: matches the first child element
`div:nth-child(2)`: matches the second child element
`div:nth-child(:even)`: matches the even child elements
`div:nth-child(:odd)`: matches the odd child elements

The interesting and powerful aspect of the `nth-child()` pseudo-class is its support for linear expressions of the form an+b, where a is a positive integer and b is a non-negative integer, as shown here (using an HTML5 `<div>` element):

`div:nth-child(3n)`: matches every third child, starting from position 0
`div:nth-child(3n+1)`: matches every third child, starting from position 1
`div:nth-child(3n+2)`: matches every third child, starting from position 2

CSS3 Attribute Selection

You can specify CSS3 selectors that select HTML elements as well as HTML elements based on the value of an attribute of an HTML element using various regular expressions. For example, the following selector selects `img` elements whose `src` attribute starts with the text string `Laurie`, and then sets the `width` attribute and the `height` attribute of the selected `img` elements to `100px`:

```
img[src^="Laurie"] {
    width: 100px; height: 100px;
}
```

The preceding CSS3 selector is useful when you want to set different dimensions to images based on the name of the images (`Laurie`, `Shelly`, `Steve`, and so forth).

The following HTML `<img>` elements do not match the preceding selector:

```
<img src="3Laurie" width="200" height="200" />
<img src="3Laurrie" width="200" height="200" />
```

The following selector selects HTML img elements whose src attribute ends with the text string jpeg, and then sets the width attribute and the height attribute of the selected img elements to 150px:

```
img[src$="jpeg"] {
    width: 150px; height: 150px;
}
```

The preceding CSS3 selector is useful when you want to set different dimensions to images based on the type of the images (jpg, png, jpeg, and so forth).

The following selector selects HTML img elements whose src attribute contains any occurrence of the text string baby, and then sets the width attribute and the height attribute of the selected HTML img elements to 200px:

```
img[src*="baby"] {
    width: 200px; height: 200px;
}
```

The preceding CSS3 selector is useful when you want to set different dimensions to images based on the "classification" of the images (mybaby, yourbaby, babygirl, babyboy, and so forth).

If you want to learn more about patterns (and their descriptions) that you can use in CSS3 selectors, an extensive list is available here:

http://www.w3.org/TR/css3-selectors

This concludes the first part of this chapter. The next section delves into CSS3 graphics-oriented effects, such as rounded corners and shadow effects.

CSS3 SHADOW EFFECTS AND ROUNDED CORNERS

CSS3 shadow effects are useful for creating vivid visual effects. You can use shadow effects for text as well as rectangular regions. CSS3 also enables you to easily render rectangles with rounded corners, so you do not need JPG files in order to create this effect.

Specifying Colors with RGB and HSL

Before we delve into the interesting features of CSS3, you need to know how to represent colors. One method is to use (R,G,B) triples, which represent the Red, Green, and Blue components of a color. For instance, the triples (255,0,0), (255,255,0), and (0,0,255) represent the colors Red, Yellow, and Blue. Other ways of specifying the color include: the hexadecimal triples (FF, 0, 0) and (FF, 0, 0); the decimal triple (100%,0,0); or the string #F00. You can also use (R,G,B,A), where the fourth component specifies the opacity, which is a decimal number between 0 (invisible) to 1 (opaque) inclusive.

However, there is also the HSL (Hue, Saturation, and Luminosity) representation of colors, where the first component is an angle between 0 and 360 (0 degrees is north), and the other two components are percentages between 0 and 100. For instance, (0,100%,50%), (120, 100%, 50%), and (240, 100%, 50%) represent the colors Red, Green, and Blue, respectively.

The code samples in this book use (R,G,B) and (R,G,B,A) for representing colors, but you can perform an Internet search to obtain more information regarding HSL.

CSS3 and Text Shadow Effects

A shadow effect for text can make a web page look more vivid and appealing, and many Web sites look better with shadow effects that are not overpowering for users (unless you specifically need to create such effects).

Listing 2.1 displays the contents of the HTML5 page TextShadow1.html that illustrate how to render text with a shadow effect, and Listing 2.2 displays the contents of the CSS stylesheet TextShadow1.css that is referenced in Listing 2.1.

LISTING 2.1 TextShadow1.html

```
<!DOCTYPE html>
<html lang="en">
<head>
  <meta charset="utf-8" />
  <title>CSS Text Shadow Example</title>
  <link href="TextShadow1.css" rel="stylesheet" type="text/css">
</head>

<body>
  <div id="text1">Line One Shadow Effect</div>
  <div id="text2">Line Two Shadow Effect</div>
  <div id="text3">Line Three Vivid Effect</div>
  <div id="text4">
    <span id="dd">13</span>
    <span id="mm">August</span>
    <span id="yy">2012</span>
  </div>
  <div id="text5">
    <span id="dd">13</span>
    <span id="mm">August</span>
    <span id="yy">2012</span>
  </div>
  <div id="text6">
    <span id="dd">13</span>
    <span id="mm">August</span>
    <span id="yy">2012</span>
  </div>
</body>
</html>
```

The code in Listing 2.1 is straightforward: there is a reference to the CSS stylesheet `TextShadow1.css` that contains two CSS selectors. One selector specifies how to render the HTML `<div>` element whose id attribute has value `text1`, and the other selector matches the HTML `<div>` element whose id attribute is `text2`. Although the CSS3 `rotate()` function is included in this example, we'll defer a more detailed discussion of this function until later in this chapter.

LISTING 2.2 TextShadow1.css

```
#text1 {
  font-size: 24pt;
  text-shadow: 2px 4px 5px #00f;
}


#text2 {
  font-size: 32pt;
  text-shadow: 0px 1px 6px #000,
               4px 5px 6px #f00;
}
/* note the multiple parts in the text-shadow definition */
#text3 {
  font-size: 40pt;
  text-shadow: 0px 1px 6px  #fff,
               2px 4px 4px  #0ff,
               4px 5px 6px  #00f,
               0px 0px 10px #444,
               0px 0px 20px #844,
               0px 0px 30px #a44,
               0px 0px 40px #f44;
}

#text4 {
  position: absolute;
  top: 200px;
  right: 200px;
  font-size: 48pt;
  text-shadow: 0px 1px 6px  #fff,
               2px 4px 4px  #0ff,
               4px 5px 6px  #00f,
               0px 0px 10px #000,
               0px 0px 20px #448,
               0px 0px 30px #a4a,
               0px 0px 40px #fff;
  -webkit-transform: rotate(-90deg);
}

#text5 {
  position: absolute;
  left: 0px;
  font-size: 48pt;
  text-shadow: 2px 4px 5px #00f;
  -webkit-transform: rotate(-10deg);
}
```

```
#text6 {
  float: left;
  font-size: 48pt;
  text-shadow: 2px 4px 5px #f00;
  -webkit-transform: rotate(-170deg);
}

/* 'transform' is explained later */
#text1:hover, #text2:hover, #text3:hover,
#text4:hover, #text5:hover, #text6:hover {
  -webkit-transform : scale(2) rotate(-45deg);
  -transform : scale(2) rotate(-45deg);
}
```

The first selector in Listing 2.2 specifies a `font-size` of 24 and a `text-shadow` that renders text with a blue background (represented by the hexadecimal value `#00f`). The attribute `text-shadow` specifies (from left to right) the x-coordinate, the y-coordinate, the blur radius, and the color of the shadow. The second selector specifies a `font-size` of 32 and a red shadow background (`#f00`). The third selector creates a richer visual effect by specifying multiple components in the `text-shadow` property, which were chosen by experimenting with effects that are possible with different values in the various components.

The final CSS3 selector creates an animation effect whenever users hover over any of the six text strings; the details of the animation will be deferred until later in this chapter.

Figure 2.1 displays the result of matching the selectors in the CSS stylesheet `TextShadow1.css` with the HTML `<div>` elements in the HTML page `TextShadow1.html`. The landscape-mode screenshot is taken from an Android application (based on the code in Listing 2.1 and Listing 2.2) running on a Nexus S 4G (Android ICS) smartphone.

FIGURE 2.1 CSS3 Text shadow effects

CSS3 and Box Shadow Effects

You can also apply a shadow effect to a box that encloses a text string, which can be effective in terms of drawing attention to specific parts of a Web page. However, the same caveat regarding over-use applies to box shadows.

The HTML page `BoxShadow1.html` and `BoxShadow1.css` are not shown here but they are available on the DVD, and together they render a box shadow effect.

The key property is the `box-shadow` property, as shown here in bold for Mozilla, `WebKit`, and the non-prefixed property:

```
#box1 {
  position:relative;top:10px;
  width: 50%;
```

```
height: 30px;
font-size: 20px;
-moz-box-shadow: 10px 10px 5px #800;
-webkit-box-shadow: 10px 10px 5px #800;
box-shadow: 10px 10px 5px #800;
```

Figure 2.2 displays a landscape-mode screenshot is taken from a Nexus S 4G with Android ICS (based on the code in BoxShadow1.html and BoxShadow1.css).

CSS3 and Rounded Corners

Web developers have waited a long time for rounded corners in CSS, and CSS3 makes it very easy to render boxes with rounded corners. Listing 2.3 displays the contents of the HTML page RoundedCorners1.html that renders text strings in boxes with rounded corners, and Listing 2.4 displays the CSS file RoundedCorners1.css.

LISTING 2.3 RoundedCorners1.html

```html
<!DOCTYPE html>
<html lang="en">
<head>
    <link href="RoundedCorners1.css" rel="stylesheet" type="text/
css">
</head>
<body>
  <div id="outer">
    <a href="#" class="anchor">Text Inside a Rounded Rectangle</a>
  </div>
  <div id="text1">Line One of Text with a Shadow Effect</div>
  <div id="text2">Line Two of Text with a Shadow Effect</div>
```

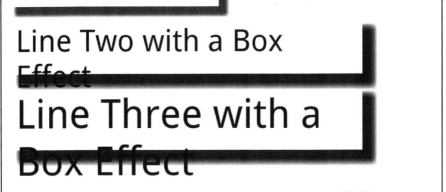

FIGURE 2.2 CSS3 box shadow effect on a Sprint Nexus with Android ICS

```
</body>
</html>
```

Listing 2.3 contains a reference to the CSS stylesheet `Rounded-Corners1.css` that contains three CSS selectors that match the elements whose `id` attribute has value `anchor`, `text1`, and `text2`, respectively. The CSS selectors defined in `RoundedCorners1.css` create visual effects, and as you will see, the `hover` pseudo-selector enables you to create animation effects.

LISTING 2.4 RoundedCorners1.css
```
a.anchor:hover {
background: #00F;
}

a.anchor {
background: #FF0;
font-size: 24px;
font-weight: bold;
padding: 4px 4px;
color: rgba(255,0,0,0.8);
text-shadow: 0 1px 1px rgba(0,0,0,0.4);
-webkit-transition: all 2.0s ease;
-transition: all 2.0s ease;
-webkit-border-radius: 8px;
border-radius: 8px;
}
```

Listing 2.4 contains the selector `a.anchor:hover` that changes the text color from yellow (`#FF0`) to blue (`#00F`) during a two-second interval whenever users hover over any anchor element with their mouse.

The selector `a.anchor` contains various attributes that specify the dimensions of the box that encloses the text in the `<a>` element, along with two new pairs of attributes. The first pair specifies the `transition` attribute (and a `WebKit`-specific prefix), which we will discuss later in this chapter. The second pair specifies the `border-radius` attribute (and the `WebKit`-specific attribute) whose value is `8px`, which determines the radius (in pixels) of the rounded corners of the box that encloses the text in the `<a>` element. The last two selectors are identical to the selectors in Listing 2.1.

Figure 2.3 displays the result of matching the selectors that are defined in the CSS stylesheet `RoundedCorners1.css` with elements in the HTML page `RoundedCorners1.html` in a landscape-mode screenshot taken from an Asus Prime tablet with Android ICS.

CSS3 GRADIENTS

CSS3 supports linear gradients and radial gradients, which enable you to create gradient effects that are as visually rich as gradients in other technologies such as SVG. The code samples in this section illustrate how to define

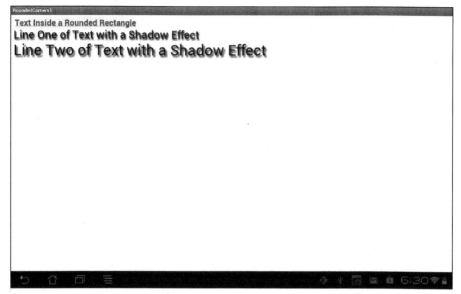

FIGURE 2.3 CSS3 rounded corners effect on an Asus Prime Tablet with Android ICS

linear gradients and radial gradients in CSS3 and then match them to HTML elements.

Linear Gradients

CSS3 linear gradients require you to specify one or more "color stops," each of which specifies a start color, an end color, and a rendering pattern. `Webkit`-based browsers support the following syntax to define a linear gradient:

- A start point
- An end point
- A start color using `from()`
- Zero or more stop-colors
- An end color using `to()`

A start point can be specified as an `(x,y)` pair of numbers or percentages. For example, the pair `(100,25%)` specifies the point that is `100` pixels to the right of the origin and `25%` of the way down from the top of the pattern. Recall that the origin is located in the upper-left corner of the screen.

Listing 2.5 displays the contents of `LinearGradient1.html` and Listing 2.6 displays the contents of `LinearGradient1.css`, which illustrate how to use linear gradients with text strings that are enclosed in `<p>` elements and an `<h3>` element.

LISTING 2.5 LinearGradient1.html

```
<!doctype html>
<html lang="en">
```

```
<head>
  <meta charset="utf-8" />
  <title>CSS Linear Gradient Example</title>
  <link href="LinearGradient1.css" rel="stylesheet" type="text/css">
</head>

<body>
  <div id="outer">
    <p id="line1">line 1 with a linear gradient</p>
    <p id="line2">line 2 with a linear gradient</p>
    <p id="line3">line 3 with a linear gradient</p>
    <p id="line4">line 4 with a linear gradient</p>
    <p id="outline">line 5 with Shadow Outline</p>
    <h3><a href="#">A Line of Gradient Text</a></h3>
  </div>
</body>
</html>
```

Listing 2.5 is a simple Web page containing four <p> elements and one <h3> element. Listing 2.5 also references the CSS stylesheet LinearGradient1.css that contains CSS selectors that match the four <p> elements and the <h3> element in Listing 2.5.

LISTING 2.6 LinearGradient1.css

```
#line1 {
width: 50%;
font-size: 32px;
background-image: -webkit-gradient(linear, 0% 0%, 0% 100%,
                                   from(#fff), to(#f00));
background-image: -gradient(linear, 0% 0%, 0% 100%,
                            from(#fff), to(#f00));
-webkit-border-radius: 4px;
border-radius: 4px;
}

#line2 {
width: 50%;
font-size: 32px;
background-image: -webkit-gradient(linear, 100% 0%, 0% 100%,
                                   from(#fff), to(#ff0));
background-image: -gradient(linear, 100% 0%, 0% 100%,
                            from(#fff), to(#ff0));
-webkit-border-radius: 4px;
border-radius: 4px;
}

#line3 {
width: 50%;
font-size: 32px;
background-image: -webkit-gradient(linear, 0% 0%, 0% 100%,
                                   from(#f00), to(#00f));
background-image: -gradient(linear, 0% 0%, 0% 100%,
                            from(#f00), to(#00f));
-webkit-border-radius: 4px;
border-radius: 4px;
}
```

```
#line4 {
width: 50%;
font-size: 32px;
background-image: -webkit-gradient(linear, 100% 0%, 0% 100%,
                           from(#f00), to(#00f));
background-image: -gradient(linear, 100% 0%, 0% 100%,
                           from(#f00), to(#00f));
-webkit-border-radius: 4px;
border-radius: 4px;
}

#outline {
font-size: 2.0em;
font-weight: bold;
color: #fff;
text-shadow: 1px 1px 1px rgba(0,0,0,0.5);
}

h3 {
width: 50%;
position: relative;
margin-top: 0;
font-size: 32px;
font-family: helvetica, ariel;
}

h3 a {
position: relative;
color: red;
text-decoration: none;
-webkit-mask-image: -webkit-gradient(linear, left top, left bottom,
                         from(rgba(0,0,0,1)),
                      color-stop(50%, rgba(0,0,0,0.5)),
                         to(rgba(0,0,0,0))));
}

h3:after {
content:"This is a Line of Gradient Text";
color: blue;
}
```

The first selector in Listing 2.6 specifies a font-size of 32 for text, a border-radius of 4 (which renders rounded corners), and a linear gradient that varies from white to blue, as shown here:

```
#line1 {
width: 50%;
font-size: 32px;
background-image: -webkit-gradient(linear, 0% 0%, 0% 100%,
                           from(#fff), to(#f00));
background-image: -gradient(linear, 0% 0%, 0% 100%,
                           from(#fff), to(#f00));
-webkit-border-radius: 4px;
border-radius: 4px;
}
```

As you can see, the first selector contains two attributes with a `-webkit-` prefix and two standard attributes without this prefix. Since the next three selectors in Listing 2.6 are similar to the first selector, we will not discuss their content.

The next CSS selector creates a text outline with a nice shadow effect by rendering the text in white with a thin black shadow, as shown here:

```
color: #fff;
text-shadow: 1px 1px 1px rgba(0,0,0,0.5);
```

The final portion of Listing 2.6 contains three selectors that affect the rendering of the `<h3>` element and its embedded `<a>` element: the h3 selector specifies the width and font size; the `the h3 a selector` specifies a `linear gradient`; and the h3:after selector specifies the text string "This is a Line of Gradient Text" to display *after* the HTML5 `<h3>` element (you can use h3:before to specify a text string to display *before* an HTML5 `<h3>` element). Other attributes are specified, but these are the main attributes for these selectors.

Figure 2.4 displays the result of matching the selectors in the CSS stylesheet `LinearGradient1.css` to the HTML page `LinearGradient1.html` in a landscape-mode screenshot taken from an Android application running on an Asus Prime tablet with Android ICS.

Radial Gradients

CSS3 radial gradients are more complex than CSS3 linear gradients, but you can use them to create more complex gradient effects. `Webkit`-based browsers support the following syntax to define a radial gradient:

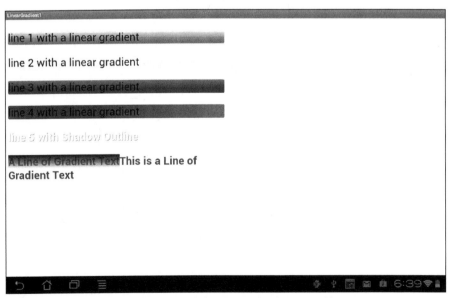

Figure 2.4 CSS3 linear gradient effect on an Asus Prime Android ICS 10" tablet

- A start point
- A start radius
- An end point
- An end radius
- A start color using `from()`
- Zero or more color-stops
- An end color using `to()`

Notice that the syntax for a radial gradient is similar to the syntax for a linear gradient, except that you also specify a start radius and an end radius.

The HTML5 Web page `RadialGradient1.html` and the CSS stylesheet `RadialGradient1.css` are not shown here, but the full listing is available on the DVD. The essence of the code in the HTML5 code involves this code block:

```
<div id="outer">
  <div id="radial3">Text3</div>
  <div id="radial2">Text2</div>
  <div id="radial4">Text4</div>
  <div id="radial1">Text1</div>
</div>
```

The CSS stylesheet `RadialGradient1.css` contains five CSS selectors that match the five HTML `<div>` elements, and one of the selectors is shown here:

```
#radial1 {
background: -webkit-gradient(
  radial, 500 40%, 0, 301 25%, 360, from(red),
  color-stop(0.05, orange), color-stop(0.4, yellow),
  color-stop(0.6, green), color-stop(0.8, blue),
  to(#fff)
 );
}
```

The `#radial1` selector contains a `background` attribute that defines a radial gradient using the `-webkit-` prefix, and it specifies the following:

- A start point of (500, 40%)
- A start radius of 0
- An end point of (301, 25%)
- An end radius of 360
- A start color of red
- An end color of white (`#fff`)

The other selectors have the same syntax as the first selector, but the rendered radial gradients are significantly different. You can create these (and other) effects by specifying different start points and end points, and by specifying a start radius that is larger than the end radius.

Figure 2.5 displays the result of matching the selectors in the CSS stylesheet `RadialGradient1.css` to the HTML page `RadialGradient1.html` in a landscape-mode screenshot taken from an Android application running on an Asus Prime tablet with Android ICS.

CSS3 2D TRANSFORMS

In addition to transitions, CSS3 supports four transforms that you can apply to 2D shapes and also to JPG files. The four CSS3 transforms are scale, rotate, skew, and translate. The following sections contain code samples that illustrate how to apply each of these CSS3 transforms to a set of JPG files. The animation effects occur when users hover over any of the JPG files; moreover, you can create "partial" animation effects by moving your mouse quickly between adjacent JPG files.

Listing 2.7 displays the contents of `Scale1.html` and Listing 2.8 displays the contents of `Scale1.css`, which illustrate how to scale JPG files to create a "hover box" image gallery.

LISTING 2.7 Scale1.html

```
<!DOCTYPE html>
<html lang="en">
<head>
  <meta charset="utf-8" />
  <title>CSS Scale Transform Example</title>
  <link href="Scale1.css" rel="stylesheet" type="text/css">
</head>

<body>
```

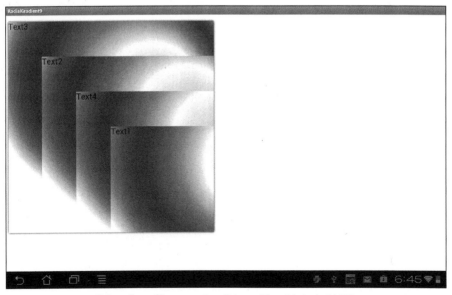

FIGURE 2.5 CSS3 radial gradient effect on an Asus Prime tablet with Android ICS

```
<header><h1>Hover Over any of the Images:</h1></header>

<div id="outer">
 <img src="Lauriel.jpeg" class="scaled" width="150" height="150"/>
 <img src="Laurie2.jpeg" class="scaled" width="150" height="150"/>
 <img src="Lauriel.jpeg" class="scaled" width="150" height="150"/>
 <img src="Laurie2.jpeg" class="scaled" width="150" height="150"/>
 </div>
</body>
</html>
```

Listing 2.7 references the CSS stylesheet Scale1.css (which contains selectors for creating scaled effects) and four HTML <img> elements that references the JPG files Lauriel.jpeg and Laurie2.jpeg. The remainder of Listing 2.7 is straightforward, with simple boilerplate text and HTML elements.

LISTING 2.8 Scale1.css

```
#outer {
float: left;
position: relative; top: 50px; left: 50px;
}
img {
-webkit-transition: -webkit-transform 1.0s ease;
-transition: transform 1.0s ease;
}

img.scaled {
  -webkit-box-shadow: 10px 10px 5px #800;
  box-shadow: 10px 10px 5px #800;
}

img.scaled:hover {
-webkit-transform : scale(2);
-transform : scale(2);
}
```

The img selector in Listing 2.8 contains specifies a transition property that applies a transform effect that occurs during a one-second interval using the ease function, as shown here:

```
-transition: transform 1.0s ease;
```

Next, the selector img.scaled specifies a box-shadow property that creates a reddish shadow effect (which you saw earlier in this chapter), as shown here:

```
img.scaled {
  -webkit-box-shadow: 10px 10px 5px #800;
  box-shadow: 10px 10px 5px #800;
}
```

Finally, the selector `img.scaled:hover` specifies a `transform` attribute that uses the `scale()` function in order to double the size of the associated JPG file whenever users hover over any of the `<img>` elements with their mouse, as shown here:

```
-transform : scale(2);
```

Since the `img` selector specifies a one-second interval using an `ease` function, the scaling effect will last for one second. Experiment with different values for the CSS3 `scale()` function and also different value for the time interval to create the animation effects that suit your needs.

Another point to remember is that you can scale both horizontally and vertically:

```
img {
-webkit-transition: -webkit-transform 1.0s ease;
-transition: transform 1.0s ease;
}

img.mystyle:hover {
-webkit-transform : scaleX(1.5) scaleY(0.5);
-transform : scaleX(1.5) scaleY(0.5);
}
```

Figure 2.6 displays the result of matching the selectors in the CSS stylesheet `Scale1.css` to the HTML page `Scale1.html`. The landscape-mode screenshot is taken from an Android application (based on the code in Listing 2.7 and Listing 2.8) running on a Nexus S 4G smartphone with Android ICS.

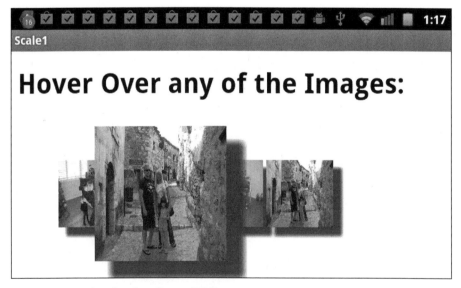

FIGURE 2.6 CSS3-based scaling effect on JPG files

Rotate Transforms

The CSS3 `transform` attribute allows you to specify the `rotate()` function in order to create scaling effects, and its syntax looks like this:

```
rotate(someValue);
```

You can replace `someValue` with any number. When `someValue` is positive, the rotation is clockwise; when `someValue` is negative, the rotation is counter clockwise; and when `someValue` is zero, there is no rotation effect. In all cases, the initial position for the rotation effect is the positive horizontal axis.

The HTML5 Web page `Rotate1.html` and the CSS stylesheet `Rotate1.css` on the DVD illustrate how to create rotation effects, a sample of which is shown here:

```
img.imageL:hover {
-webkit-transform : scale(2) rotate(-45deg);
-transform : scale(2) rotate(-45deg);
}
```

The `img` selector that specifies a `transition` attribute that creates an animation effect during a one-second interval using the `ease` timing function, as shown here:

```
-transition: transform 1.0s ease;
```

The CSS3 transform attribute allows you to specify the `skew()` function in order to create skewing effects, and its syntax looks like this:

```
skew(xAngle, yAngle);
```

You can replace `xAngle` and `yAngle` with any number. When `xAngle` and `yAngle` are positive, the skew effect is clockwise; when `xAngle` and `yAngle` are negative, the skew effect is counter clockwise; and when `xAngle` and `yAngle` are zero, there is no skew effect. In all cases, the initial position for the skew effect is the positive horizontal axis.

The HTML5 Web page `Skew1.html` and the CSS stylesheet `Skew1.css` are on the DVD, and they illustrate how to create skew effects. The CSS stylesheet contains the `img` selector, which specifies a `transition` attribute that creates an animation effect during a one-second interval using the `ease` timing function, as shown here:

```
-transition: transform 1.0s ease;
```

The four selectors `img.skewed1`, `img.skewed2`, `img.skewed3`, and `img.skewed4` create background shadow effects with darker shades of red, yellow, green, and blue, respectively (all of which you have seen in earlier code samples).

The selector `img.skewed1:hover` specifies a transform attribute that performs a skew effect whenever users hover over the first `<img>` element with their mouse, as shown here:

```
-transform : scale(2) skew(-10deg, -30deg);
```

The other three CSS3 selectors also use a combination of the CSS functions `skew()` and `scale()` to create distinct visual effects. Notice that the fourth hover selector also sets the `opacity` property to `0.5`, which takes place in parallel with the other effects in this selector.

Figure 2.7 displays the result of matching the selectors in the CSS stylesheet `Skew1.css` to the elements in the HTML page `Skew1.html`. The landscape-mode screenshot is taken from an Android application running on a Nexus S 4G smartphone with Android ICS.

The CSS3 transform attribute allows you to specify the `translate()` function in order to create an effect that involves a horizontal and/or vertical "shift" of an element, and its syntax looks like this:

```
translate(xDirection, yDirection);
```

The translation is in relation to the origin, which is the upper-left corner of the screen. Thus, positive values for `xDirection` and `yDirection` produce a shift toward the right and a shift downward, respectively, whereas negative values for `xDirection` and `yDirection` produce a shift toward the left and a shift upward; zero values for `xDirection` and `yDirection` do not cause any translation effect.

The Web page `Translate1.html` and the CSS stylesheet `Translate1.css` on the DVD illustrate how to apply a translation effect to a JPG file.

FIGURE 2.7 CSS3-based skew effects on JPG files

```
img.trans2:hover {
-webkit-transform : scale(0.5) translate(-50px, -50px);
-transform : scale(0.5) translate(-50px, -50px);
}
```

The CSS stylesheet contains the `img` selector specifies a transform effect during a one-second interval using the `ease` timing function, as shown here:

```
-transition: transform 1.0s ease;
```

The four selectors `img.trans1`, `img.trans2`, `img.trans3`, and `img.trans4` create background shadow effects with darker shades of red, yellow, green, and blue, respectively, just as you saw in the previous section.

The selector `img.trans1:hover` specifies a `transform` attribute that performs a scale effect and a translation effect whenever users hover over the first `<img>` element with their mouse, as shown here:

```
-webkit-transform : scale(2) translate(100px, 50px);
transform : scale(2) translate(100px, 50px);
```

Figure 2.8 displays the result of matching the selectors defined in the CSS3 stylesheet `Translate1.css` to the elements in the HTML page `Translate1.html`. The landscape-mode screenshot is taken from an Android application running on a Nexus S 4G smartphone with Android ICS.

CSS3 MEDIA QUERIES

CSS3 media queries are very useful logical expressions that enable you detect mobile applications on devices with differing physical attributes and orientation. For example, with CSS3 media queries you can change the dimensions and layout of your applications so that they render appropriately on smart phones as well as tablets.

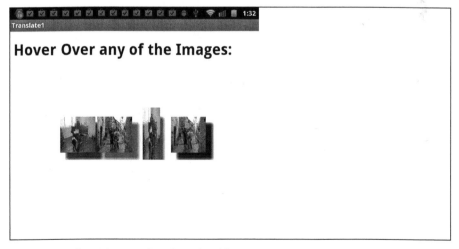

Figure 2.8 JPG files with css3 scale and translate effects

Specifically, you can use CSS3 media queries in order to determine the following characteristics of a device:

- Browser window width and height
- Device width and height
- Orientation (landscape or portrait)
- Aspect ratio
- Device aspect ratio
- Resolution

CSS3 media queries are Boolean expressions that contain one or more "simple terms" (connected with and or or) that evaluate to true or false. Thus, CSS3 media queries represent conditional logic that evaluates to either true or false.

As an example, the following link element loads the CSS stylesheet mystuff.css only if the device is a screen and the maximum width of the device is 480px:

```
<link rel="stylesheet" type="text/css"
      media="screen and (max-device-width: 480px)" href="mystuff.
css"/>
```

The preceding link contains a media attribute that specifies two components: a media type of screen and a query that specifies a max-device-width whose value is 480px. The supported values for media in CSS3 media queries are braille, embossed, handheld, print, projection, screen, speech, tty, and tv.

The next CSS3 media query checks the media type, the maximum device width, and the resolution of a device:

```
@media screen and (max-device-width: 480px) and (resolution:
160dpi) {
  #innerDiv {
    float: none;
  }
}
```

If the CSS3 media query in the preceding code snippet evaluates to true, then the nested CSS selector will match the HTML element whose id attribute has the value innerDiv, and its float property will be set to none on any device whose maximum screen width is 480px. As you can see, it's possible to create compact CSS3 media queries that contain non-trivial logic, which is obviously very useful because CSS3 does not have any if/then/else construct that is available in other programming languages.

ADDITIONAL CODE SAMPLES

The CSS stylesheet CSS3MediaQuery1.css and the HTML5 Web page CSS3MediaQuery1.html (both are on the DVD) illustrate how to use media queries in order to change the size of two images when users rotate their mobile device.

You can detect a change of orientation of a mobile device using simple Java-Script code, so you are not "forced" to use CSS3 media queries. The HTML5 Web page CSS3OrientationJS1.html on the DVD illustrates how to use standard JavaScript in order to change the size of two images when users rotate their mobile device.

In essence, the code uses the value of the variable window.orientation in order to detect four different orientations of your mobile device, and in each of those four cases, the dimensions of the JPG files are updated with the following type of code:

```
document.getElementById("img1").style.width  = "120px";
document.getElementById("img1").style.height = "300px";
```

Although this is a very simple example, hopefully this code gives you an appreciation for the capabilities of CSS3 media queries.

SUMMARY

This chapter showed you how to create graphics effects, shadow effects, and how to use CSS3 transforms in CSS3. You learned how to create animation effects that you can apply to HTML elements, and you saw how to define CSS3 selectors to do the following:

- Render rounded rectangles
- Create shadow effects for text and 2D shapes
- Create linear and radial gradients
- Use the methods translate(), rotate(), skew(), and scale()
- Create CSS3-based animation effects

SVG ESSENTIALS

This chapter gives you an overview of SVG, along with examples of how to reference SVG documents in CSS3 selectors. Keep in mind that the CSS3 examples in this book are for WebKit-based browsers, but you can insert the CSS3 code for other browsers by using browser-specific prefixes (which were discussed briefly in Chapter 2).

The majority of this chapter delves into SVG, which is an XML-based technology for rendering 2D shapes. SVG supports linear gradients, radial gradients, filter effects, transforms (translate, scale, skew, and rotate), and animation effects using an XML-based syntax. Although SVG does not support 3D effects, SVG provides functionality that is unavailable in CSS3, such as support for arbitrary polygons, elliptic arcs, and quadratic and cubic Bezier curves.

Fortunately, you can reference SVG documents in CSS selectors, and the combination of CSS3 and SVG gives you a powerful mechanism for leveraging the functionality of SVG in CSS3 selectors. In this chapter, the screenshots of Android ICS mobile applications on an Asus Prime Android ICS 10" tablet explicitly use Android ICS. If you plan on developing Android-based mobile applications with SVG, keep in mind that although Android ICS does support most SVG features, there is no support for SVG filters.

OVERVIEW OF SVG

This section of the chapter contains various examples that illustrate some of the 2D shapes and effects that you can create with SVG. In addition to the compressed overview of SVG outlined here, you can search the Internet for SVG books and online tutorials, and explore the following open source projects:

http://code.google.com/p/svg-graphics/
http://code.google.com/p/svg-filters-graphics/

Basic 2D Shapes in SVG

This section shows you how to render line segments and rectangles in SVG documents. As a simple example, SVG supports a `<line>` element for rendering line segments, and its syntax looks like this:

```
<line x1="20" y1="20" x2="100" y2="150".../>
```

An SVG `<line>` elements render line segments that connect the two points (x1,y1) and (x2,y2).

SVG supports a `<rect>` element for rendering rectangles, and its syntax looks like this:

```
<rect width="200" height="50" x="20" y="50".../>
```

The SVG `<rect>` element renders a rectangle whose width and height are specified in the `width` and `height` attributes. The upper-left vertex of the rectangle is specified by the point with coordinates (x,y).

Listing 3.1 displays the contents of `BasicShapes1.svg` that illustrates how to render line segments and rectangles.

LISTING 3.1 BasicShapes1.svg

```
<?xml version="1.0" encoding="iso-8859-1"?>
<!DOCTYPE svg PUBLIC "-//W3C//DTD SVG 20001102//EN"
 "http://www.w3.org/TR/2000/CR-SVG-20001102/DTD/svg-20001102.dtd">

<svg xmlns="http://www.w3.org/2000/svg"
     xmlns:xlink="http://www.w3.org/1999/xlink"
     width="100%" height="100%">
 <g>
  <!-- left-side figures -->
  <line x1="20" y1="20" x2="220" y2="20"
        stroke="blue" stroke-width="4"/>

  <line x1="20" y1="40" x2="220" y2="40"
        stroke="red" stroke-width="10"/>

  <rect width="200" height="50" x="20" y="70"
        fill="red" stroke="black" stroke-width="4"/>

  <path d="M20,150 l200,0 10,50 l-200,0 z"
        fill="blue" stroke="red" stroke-width="4"/>

  <!-- right-side figures -->
  <path d="M250,20 l200,0 l-100,50 z"
        fill="blue" stroke="red" stroke-width="4"/>

  <path d="M300,100 l100,0 l50,50 l-50,50 l-100,0 l-50,-50 z"
        fill="yellow" stroke="red" stroke-width="4"/>
 </g>
</svg>
```

The first SVG `<line>` element in Listing 3.1 specifies the color `blue` and a `stroke-width` (i.e., the width of the line segment) of `4`, whereas the second SVG `<line>` element specifies the color `red` and a `stroke-width` of `10`. You can also use other formats for colors. For example, `#f00` and `rgb(f,0,0)` are two other ways to specify the color `red`.

Notice that the first SVG `<rect>` element renders a rectangle that looks the same (except for the color) as the second SVG `<line>` element, which shows that it's possible to use different SVG elements to render a rectangle (or a line segment).

The SVG `<path>` element is probably the most flexible and powerful element because you can create arbitrarily complex shapes based on a "concatenation" of other SVG elements. Later in this chapter, you will see an example of how to render multiple Bezier curves in an SVG `<path>` element.

An SVG `<path>` element contains a `d` attribute that specifies the points in the desired path. For example, the first SVG `<path>` element in Listing 3.1 contains the following `d` attribute:

```
d="M20,150 1200,0 10,50 1-200,0 z"
```

This is how to interpret the contents of the `d` attribute:

- Move to the absolute location point (`20,150`)
- Draw a horizontal line segment `200` pixels to the right
- Draw a line segment by moving `10` pixels to the right and `50` pixels down
- Draw a horizontal line segment by moving `200` pixels toward the left
- Draw a line segment to the initial point (specified by `z`)

Similar comments apply to the other two SVG `<path>` elements in Listing 3.1. One thing to keep in mind is that uppercase letters (`C`, `L`, `M`, and `Q`) refer to absolute positions whereas lowercase letters (`c`, `l`, `m`, and `q`) refer to relative positions with respect to the element that is to the immediate left. Experiment with the code in Listing 3.1 by using combinations of lowercase and uppercase letters to gain a better understanding of how to create different visual effects.

Figure 3.1 displays the result of rendering the SVG document `Basic-Shapes1.svg`, in a landscape-mode screenshot taken from an Android application running on an Asus Prime Android ICS 10" tablet.

SVG Gradients and the `<path>` Element

As you have probably surmised, SVG supports linear gradients and radial gradients that you can apply to 2D shapes. For example, you can use the SVG `<path>` element to define elliptic arcs (using the `d` attribute) and then specify gradient effects. The SVG `<path>` element contains a `d` attribute for specifying path elements, as shown here:

```
<path d="specify a list of path elements" fill="…" />
```

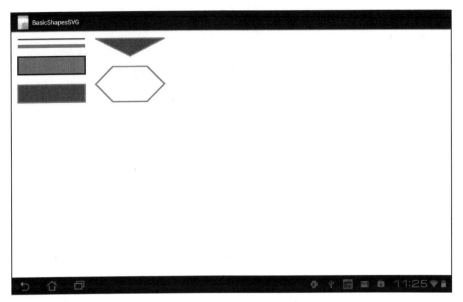

FIGURE 3.1 SVG lines and rectangles on an Asus Prime Android ICS 10" tablet

Listing 3.2 displays the contents of `BasicShapesLRG1.svg` that illustrates how to render 2D shapes with linear gradients and radial gradients.

LISTING 3.2 BasicShapesLRG1.svg

```
<?xml version="1.0" encoding="iso-8859-1"?>
<!DOCTYPE svg PUBLIC "-//W3C//DTD SVG 20001102//EN"
 "http://www.w3.org/TR/2000/CR-SVG-20001102/DTD/svg-20001102.dtd">

<svg xmlns="http://www.w3.org/2000/svg"
     xmlns:xlink="http://www.w3.org/1999/xlink"
     width="100%" height="100%">
  <defs>
    <linearGradient id="pattern1"
                    x1="0%" y1="100%" x2="100%" y2="0%">
      <stop offset="0%"    stop-color="yellow"/>
      <stop offset="40%"   stop-color="red"/>
      <stop offset="80%"   stop-color="blue"/>
    </linearGradient>

   <radialGradient id="pattern2">
      <stop offset="0%"    stop-color="yellow"/>
      <stop offset="40%"   stop-color="red"/>
      <stop offset="80%"   stop-color="blue"/>
   </radialGradient>
  </defs>


  <g>
   <ellipse cx="120" cy="80" rx="100" ry="50"
            fill="url(#pattern1)"/>

   <ellipse cx="120" cy="200" rx="100" ry="50"
```

```
              fill="url(#pattern2)"/>

    <ellipse cx="320" cy="80" rx="50" ry="50"
             fill="url(#pattern2)"/>

    <path d="M 505,145 v -100 a 250,100 0 0,1 -200,100"
          fill="black"/>

    <path d="M 500,140 v -100 a 250,100 0 0,1 -200,100"
          fill="url(#pattern1)"
          stroke="black" stroke-thickness="8"/>

    <path d="M 305,165 v  100 a 250,100 0 0,1  200,-100"
          fill="black"/>

    <path d="M 300,160 v  100 a 250,100 0 0,1  200,-100"
          fill="url(#pattern1)"
          stroke="black" stroke-thickness="8"/>

    <ellipse cx="450" cy="240" rx="50" ry="50"
             fill="url(#pattern1)"/>
  </g>
</svg>
```

Listing 3.2 contains an SVG `<defs>` element that specifies a `<linearGradient>` element (whose `id` attribute has value `pattern1`) with three stop values using an XML-based syntax, followed by a `<radialGradient>` element with three `<stop>` elements and an `id` attribute whose value is `pattern2`.

The SVG `<g>` element contains four `<ellipse>` elements, the first of which specifies the point `(120,80)` as its center `(cx,cy)`, with a major radius of `100`, a minor radius of `50`, filled with the linear gradient `pattern1`, as shown here:

```
    <ellipse cx="120" cy="80" rx="100" ry="50"
             fill="url(#pattern1)"/>
```

Similar comments apply to the other three SVG `<ellipse>` elements.

The SVG `<g>` element also contains four `<path>` elements that render elliptic arcs. The first `<path>` element specifies a black background for the elliptic arc defined with the following d attribute:

```
d="M 505,145 v -100 a 250,100 0 0,1 -200,100"
```

Unfortunately, the SVG syntax for elliptic arcs is not intuitive, and it's based the notion of major arcs and minor arcs that connect two points on an ellipse. This example is only for illustrative purposes, so we won't delve into a detailed explanation of how elliptic arcs are defined in SVG. If you need to learn the details you can perform an Internet search (and be prepared to spend some time experimenting with your own code samples).

The second SVG `<path>` element renders the same elliptic arc with a slight offset, using the linear gradient `pattern1`, which creates a shadow effect.

Similar comments apply to the other pair of SVG `<path>` elements, which render an elliptic arc with the radial gradient `pattern2` (also with a shadow effect).

Figure 3.2 displays the result of rendering `BasicShapesLRG1.svg`, in a landscape-mode screenshot taken from an Android application running on an Asus Prime Android ICS 10" tablet.

SVG <polygon> Element

The SVG `<polygon>` element contains a polygon attribute in which you can specify points that represent the vertices of a polygon. The SVG `<polygon>` element is most useful when you want to create polygons with an arbitrary number of sides, but you can also use this element to render line segments and rectangles.

The syntax of the SVG `<polygon>` element looks like this:

```
<polygon path="specify a list of points" fill="..." />
```

Listing 3.3 displays the contents of a portion of `SvgCube1.svg` that illustrates how to render a cube in SVG.

LISTING 3.3 SvgCube1.svg

```
<?xml version="1.0" encoding="iso-8859-1"?>
<!DOCTYPE svg PUBLIC "-//W3C//DTD SVG 20001102//EN"
 "http://www.w3.org/TR/2000/CR-SVG-20001102/DTD/svg-20001102.dtd">

<svg xmlns="http://www.w3.org/2000/svg"
    xmlns:xlink="http://www.w3.org/1999/xlink"
    width="100%" height="100%">
  <!-- <defs> element omitted for brevity -->
```

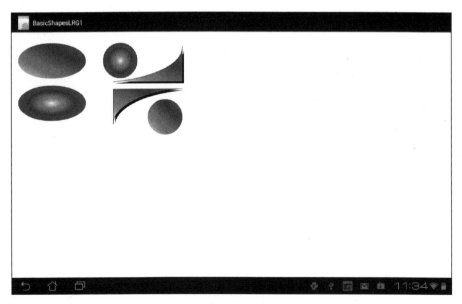

FIGURE 3.2 SVG linear radial gradient arcs on an Asus Prime Android ICS 10" tablet

```
<!-- top face (counter clockwise) -->
<polygon fill="url(#pattern1)"
         points="50,50 200,50 240,30 90,30"/>

<!-- front face -->
<rect width="150" height="150" x="50" y="50"
      fill="url(#pattern2)"/>

<!-- right face (counter clockwise) -->
<polygon fill="url(#pattern3)"
         points="200,50 200,200 240,180 240,30"/>
</svg>
```

Listing 3.3 contains an SVG `<g>` element contains the three faces of a cube, which consists of an SVG `<polygon>` element that renders the top face (which is a parallelogram), an SVG `<rect>` element that renders the front face, and another SVG `<polygon>` element that renders the right face (which is also a parallelogram). The three faces of the cube are rendered with the linear gradient and the two radial gradients defined in the SVG `<defs>` element (not shown in Listing 3.3).

Figure 3.3 displays the result of rendering the SVG document `SvgCube1.svg`, in a landscape-mode screenshot taken from an Android application running on an Asus Prime Android ICS 10" tablet.

BEZIER CURVES AND TRANSFORMS

SVG supports quadratic and cubic Bezier curves that you can render with linear gradient or radial gradients. You can also concatenate multiple Bezier

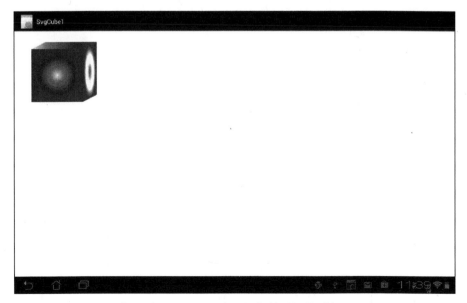

FIGURE 3.3 An SVG gradient cube on an Asus Prime Android ICS 10" tablet

curves using an SVG `<path>` element. Listing 3.4 displays the contents of
`BezierCurves1.svg` that illustrates how to render various Bezier curves.
Note that the transform-related effects are discussed later in this chapter.

LISTING 3.4 BezierCurves1.svg

```
<?xml version="1.0" encoding="iso-8859-1"?>
<!DOCTYPE svg PUBLIC "-//W3C//DTD SVG 20001102//EN"
 "http://www.w3.org/TR/2000/CR-SVG-20001102/DTD/svg-20001102.dtd">

<svg xmlns="http://www.w3.org/2000/svg"
    xmlns:xlink="http://www.w3.org/1999/xlink"
    width="100%" height="100%">
<!-- <defs> element omitted for brevity -->
<g transform="scale(1.5,0.5)">
 <path d="m 0,50 C 400,200 200,-150 100,350"
       stroke="black" stroke-width="4"
       fill="url(#pattern1)"/>
</g>

<g transform="translate(50,50)">
  <g transform="scale(0.5,1)">
   <path d="m 50,50 C 400,100 200,200 100,20"
         fill="red" stroke="black" stroke-width="4"/>
  </g>

  <g transform="scale(1,1)">
   <path d="m 50,50 C 400,100 200,200 100,20"
         fill="yellow" stroke="black" stroke-width="4"/>
  </g>
</g>

<g transform="translate(-50,50)">
  <g transform="scale(1,2)">
   <path d="M 50,50 C 400,100 200,200 100,20"
         fill="blue" stroke="black" stroke-width="4"/>
  </g>
</g>

<g transform="translate(-50,50)">
 <g transform="scale(0.5, 0.5) translate(195,345)">
  <path d="m20,20 C20,50 20,450 300,200 s-150,-250 200,100"
        fill="blue" style="stroke:#880088;stroke-width:4;"/>
 </g>

 <g transform="scale(0.5, 0.5) translate(185,335)">
  <path d="m20,20 C20,50 20,450 300,200 s-150,-250 200,100"
        fill="url(#pattern2)"
        style="stroke:#880088;stroke-width:4;"/>
 </g>

 <g transform="scale(0.5, 0.5) translate(180,330)">
  <path d="m20,20 C20,50 20,450 300,200 s-150,-250 200,100"
    fill="blue" style="stroke:#880088;stroke-width:4;"/>
 </g>

 <g transform="scale(0.5, 0.5) translate(170,320)">
```

```
    <path d="m20,20 C20,50 20,450 300,200 s-150,-250 200,100"
        fill="url(#pattern2)" style="stroke:black;stroke-width:4;"/>
    </g>
</g>

<g transform="scale(0.8,1) translate(380,120)">
 <path d="M0,0 C200,150 400,300 20,250"
        fill="url(#pattern2)" style="stroke:blue;stroke-width:4;"/>
</g>

<g transform="scale(2.0,2.5) translate(150,-80)">
 <path d="M200,150 C0,0 400,300 20,250"
        fill="url(#pattern2)" style="stroke:blue;stroke-width:4;"/>
</g>
</svg>
```

Listing 3.4 contains an SVG `<defs>` element that defines two linear gradients, followed by ten SVG `<path>` elements, each of which renders a cubic Bezier curve. The SVG `<path>` elements are enclosed in SVG `<g>` elements whose `transform` attribute contains the SVG `scale()` function or the SVG `translate()` functions (or both).

The first SVG `<g>` element invokes the SVG `scale()` function to scale the cubic Bezier curve that is specified in an SVG `<path>` element, as shown here:

```
<g transform="scale(1.5,0.5)">
 <path d="m 0,50 C 400,200 200,-150 100,350"
        stroke="black" stroke-width="4"
        fill="url(#pattern1)"/>
</g>
```

The preceding cubic Bezier curve has an initial point (0,50), with control points (400,200) and (200,-150), followed by the second control point (100,350). The Bezier curve is `black`, with a width of 4, and its `fill` attribute is the color defined in the `<linearGradient>` element (whose `id` attribute is `pattern1`) that is defined in the SVG `<defs>` element.

The remaining SVG `<path>` elements are similar to the first SVG `<path>` element, so they will not be described.

Figure 3.4 displays the result of rendering the Bezier curves that are defined in the SVG document `BezierCurves1.svg`, in a landscape-mode screenshot taken from an Android application running on an Asus Prime Android ICS 10" tablet.

SVG FILTERS, SHADOW EFFECTS, AND TEXT PATHS

You can create nice filter effects that you can apply to 2D shapes as well as text strings, and this section contains three SVG-based examples of creating such effects. Listing 3.5 displays the contents of the SVG documents `BlurFilter-Text1.svg`.

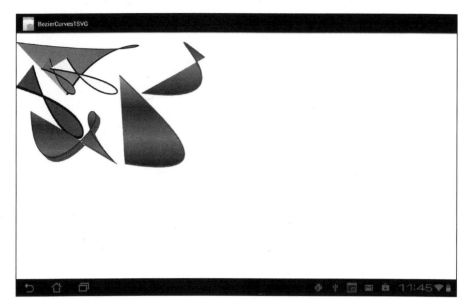

FIGURE 3.4 SVG Bezier curves on an Asus Prime Android ICS 10" tablet

LISTING 3.5 *BlurFilterText1.svg*

```
<?xml version="1.0" encoding="iso-8859-1"?>
<!DOCTYPE svg PUBLIC "-//W3C//DTD SVG 20001102//EN"
 "http://www.w3.org/TR/2000/CR-SVG-20001102/DTD/svg-20001102.dtd">

<svg xmlns="http://www.w3.org/2000/svg"
    xmlns:xlink="http://www.w3.org/1999/xlink"
    width="100%" height="100%">
  <defs>
  <filter
    id="blurFilter1"
    filterUnits="objectBoundingBox"
    x="0" y="0"
    width="100%" height="100%">
    <feGaussianBlur stdDeviation="4"/>
  </filter>
  </defs>

<g transform="translate(50,100)">
  <text id="normalText" x="0" y="0"
      fill="red" stroke="black" stroke-width="4"
      font-size="72">
    Normal Text
  </text>

  <text id="horizontalText" x="0" y="100"
      filter="url(#blurFilter1)"
      fill="red" stroke="black" stroke-width="4"
      font-size="72">
    Blurred Text
  </text>
```

```
</g>
</svg>
```

The SVG `<defs>` element in Listing 3.5 contains an SVG `<filter>` element that specifies a Gaussian blur with the following line:

```
<feGaussianBlur stdDeviation="4"/>
```

You can specify larger values for the `stdDeviation` attribute if you want to create more "diffuse" filter effects.

The first SVG `<text>` element that is contained in the SVG `<g>` element renders a normal text string, whereas the second SVG `<text>` element contains a `filter` attribute that references the filter (defined in the SVG `<defs>` element) in order to render the same text string, as shown here:

```
filter="url(#blurFilter1)"
```

Figure 3.5 displays the result of rendering `BlurFilterText1.svg` that creates a filter effect, in Google Chrome 17 on a Macbook (unfortunately, SVG filters are not rendered in Android ICS).

Listing 3.6 displays the contents of the document `TextOnQBezier-Path1.svg` that illustrates how to render a text string along the path of a quadratic Bezier curve.

LISTING 3.6 *TextOnQBezierPath1.svg*

```
<?xml version="1.0" encoding="iso-8859-1"?>
<!DOCTYPE svg PUBLIC "-//W3C//DTD SVG 20001102//EN"
 "http://www.w3.org/TR/2000/CR-SVG-20001102/DTD/svg-20001102.dtd">

<svg xmlns="http://www.w3.org/2000/svg"
     xmlns:xlink="http://www.w3.org/1999/xlink"
     width="100%" height="100%">
<defs>
  <path id="pathDefinition" d="m0,0 Q100,0 200,200 T300,200 z"/>
```

```
</defs>

<g transform="translate(100,100)">
  <text id="textStyle" fill="red"
      stroke="blue" stroke-width="2"
      font-size="24">

  <textPath xlink:href="#pathDefinition">
  Sample Text that follows a path specified by a Quadratic Bezier
curve
  </textPath>
  </text>
</g>
</svg>
```

The SVG `<defs>` element in Listing 3.6 contains an SVG `<path>` element that defines a quadratic Bezier curve (note the `Q` in the `d` attribute). This SVG `<path>` element has an `id` attribute whose value is `pathDefinition`, which is referenced later in this code sample.

The SVG `<g>` element contains an SVG `<text>` element that specifies a text string to render, as well as an SVG `<textPath>` element that specifies the path along which the text is rendered, as shown here:

```
<textPath xlink:href="#pathDefinition">
  Sample Text that follows a path specified by a Quadratic Bezier
curve
</textPath>
```

Notice that the SVG `<textPath>` element contains the attribute `xlink:href` whose value is `pathDefinition`, which is also the `id` of the SVG `<path>` element that is defined in the SVG `<defs>` element. As a result, the text string is rendered along the path of a quadratic Bezier curve instead of rendering the text string horizontally (which is the default behavior).

Figure 3.6 displays the result of rendering `TextOnQBezierPath1.svg` that renders a text string along the path of a quadratic Bezier curve, in a landscape-mode screenshot taken from an Android application running on an Asus Prime Android ICS 10" tablet.

SVG Transforms

Earlier in this chapter, you saw some examples of SVG transform effects. In addition to the SVG functions `scale()`, `translate()`, and `rotate()`, SVG provides the `skew()` function to create skew effects.

Listing 3.7 displays the contents of `TransformEffects1.svg` that illustrates how to apply transforms to rectangles and circles in SVG.

LISTING 3.7 TransformEffects1.svg
```
<?xml version="1.0" encoding="iso-8859-1"?>
<!DOCTYPE svg PUBLIC "-//W3C//DTD SVG 20001102//EN"
  "http://www.w3.org/TR/2000/CR-SVG-20001102/DTD/svg-20001102.dtd">
```

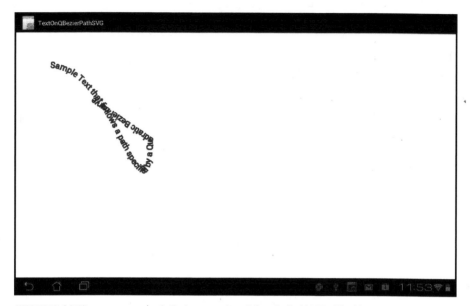

FIGURE 3.6 SVG text on a quadratic Bezier on an Asus Prime Android ICS 10" tablet

```
<svg xmlns="http://www.w3.org/2000/svg"
     xmlns:xlink="http://www.w3.org/1999/xlink"
     width="100%" height="100%">
<defs>
  <linearGradient id="gradientDefinition1"
    x1="0" y1="0" x2="200" y2="0"
    gradientUnits="userSpaceOnUse">
    <stop offset="0%"   style="stop-color:#FF0000"/>
    <stop offset="100%" style="stop-color:#440000"/>
  </linearGradient>

  <pattern id="dotPattern" width="8" height="8"
         patternUnits="userSpaceOnUse">

    <circle id="circle1" cx="2" cy="2" r="2"
       style="fill:red;"/>
  </pattern>
</defs>

<!-- full cylinder -->
<g id="largeCylinder" transform="translate(100,20)">
  <ellipse cx="0"  cy="50" rx="20" ry="50"
         stroke="blue" stroke-width="4"
         style="fill:url(#gradientDefinition1)"/>

  <rect x="0" y="0" width="300" height="100"
       style="fill:url(#gradientDefinition1)"/>

  <rect x="0" y="0" width="300" height="100"
       style="fill:url(#dotPattern)"/>

  <ellipse cx="300" cy="50" rx="20"  ry="50"
```

```
                stroke="blue" stroke-width="4"
                style="fill:yellow;"/>
</g>
<!-- half-sized cylinder -->
<g transform="translate(100,100) scale(.5)">
    <use xlink:href="#largeCylinder" x="0" y="0"/>
</g>

<!-- skewed cylinder -->
<g transform="translate(100,100) skewX(40) skewY(20)">
    <use xlink:href="#largeCylinder" x="0" y="0"/>
</g>

<!-- rotated cylinder -->
<g transform="translate(100,100) rotate(40)">
    <use xlink:href="#largeCylinder" x="0" y="0"/>
</g>
</svg>
```

The SVG `<defs>` element in Listing 3.7 contains a `<linearGradient>` element that defines a linear gradient, followed by an SVG `<pattern>` element that defines a custom pattern, which is shown here:

```
<pattern id="dotPattern" width="8" height="8"
         patternUnits="userSpaceOnUse">

    <circle id="circle1" cx="2" cy="2" r="2"
        style="fill:red;"/>
</pattern>
```

As you can see, the SVG `<pattern>` element contains an SVG `<circle>` element that is repeated in a grid-like fashion inside an 8x8 rectangle (note the values of the `width` attribute and the `height` attribute). The SVG `<pattern>` element has an `id` attribute whose value is `dotPattern` because (as you will see) this element creates a "dotted" effect.

Listing 3.7 contains four SVG `<g>` elements, each of which renders a cylinder that references the SVG `<pattern>` element that is defined in the SVG `<defs>` element.

The first SVG `<g>` element in Listing 3.7 contains two SVG `<ellipse>` elements and two SVG `<rect>` elements. The first `<ellipse>` element renders the left-side "cover" of the cylinder with the linear gradient that is defined in the SVG `<defs>` element. The first `<rect>` element renders the "body" of the cylinder with a linear gradient, and the second `<rect>` element renders the "dot pattern" on the body of the cylinder. Finally, the second `<ellipse>` element renders the right-side "cover" of the ellipse.

The other three cylinders are easy to create: they simply reference the first cylinder and apply a transformation to change the size, shape, and orientation. Specifically, these three cylinders reference the first cylinder with the following code:

```
<use xlink:href="#largeCylinder" x="0" y="0"/>
```

...and then they apply scale, skew, and rotate functions in order to render scaled, skewed, and rotated cylinders.

Figure 3.7 displays the result of rendering `TransformEffects1.svg`, in a landscape-mode screenshot taken from an Android application running on an Asus Prime Android ICS 10" tablet.

Other SVG Features

SVG supports many other features, and this section describes some of them. The referenced files are located on the DVD that accompanies this book.

SVG Animation

SVG supports animation effects that you can specify as part of the declaration of SVG elements. The SVG document `AnimateMultiRect1.svg` illustrates how to create an animation effect with four rectangles.

```
<rect id="rect1" width="100" height="100"
      stroke-width="1" stroke="blue"/>

<use xlink:href="#rect1" x="0" y="0" fill="red">
      <animate attributeName="x" attributeType="XML"
               begin="0s" dur="4s"
               fill="freeze" from="0" to="400"/>
</use>
```

The SVG `<g>` element contains an SVG `<use>` elements that perform a parallel animation effect on a rectangle. The first `<use>` element references the rectangle defined in the SVG `<defs>` element and then animates the x

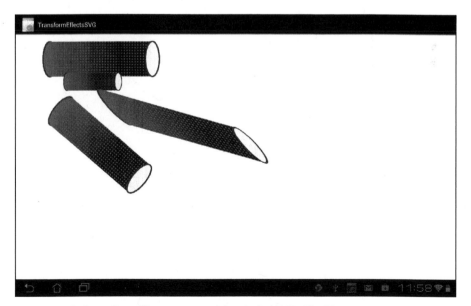

FIGURE 3.7 SVG transform effects on an Asus Prime Android ICS 10" tablet

attribute during a four-second interval. Notice that the x attribute varies from 0 to 400, which moves the rectangle horizontally from left to right. You can also animate other SVG elements, including text strings.

If you are interested in seeing how to handle zoom and pan functionality in SVG, code samples are available here:

http://msdn.microsoft.com/en-us/library/gg589508(v=vs.85).aspx

Creating 3D Effects in SVG

Although SVG does not provide 3D support, you can create 3D effects based on a combination of JavaScript and SVG. In fact, you can find an extensive set of SVG code samples illustrating 3D effects here:

http://code.google.com/p/svg-filter-graphics

Figure 3.8 displays the result of rendering `TroughPattern3S2.svg` (which is part of the preceding open source project) in a Chrome browser on a Macbook. Note that SVG filters are not supported on Android ICS.

If you are interested in creating 3D effects with SVG, you get more information (including details about matrix manipulation) and code samples here:

http://msdn.microsoft.com/en-us/library/hh535759(v=vs.85).aspx

Embedding JavaScript in SVG Documents

In addition to embedding "pure" SVG code in an HTML5 page, SVG allows you to embed JavaScript in a CDATA section to dynamically create SVG

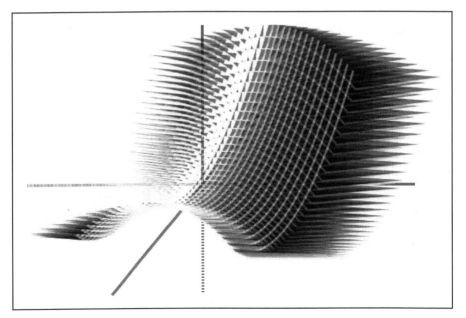

FIGURE 3.8 SVG 3D "trough" shape in a Chrome browser on a Macbook

elements and append the to the DOM of the HTML Web page. You can also define event listeners in JavaScript for SVG elements. The SVG document ArchEllipses1.svg renders a set of ellipses that follow the path of an Archimedean spiral. A fragment is shown here:

```
var svgNS = "http://www.w3.org/2000/svg";

function drawSpiral(event) {
        for(angle=0; angle<maxAngle; angle+=angleDelta) {
        ellipseNode = svgDocument.createElementNS(svgNS, "ellipse");
            ellipseNode.setAttribute("fill", redColor);
            ellipseNode.setAttribute("stroke-width", strokeWidth);
            ellipseNode.setAttribute("stroke", "yellow");

            ellipseNode.setAttribute("cx", currentX);
            ellipseNode.setAttribute("cy", currentY);
            ellipseNode.setAttribute("rx", majorAxis);
            ellipseNode.setAttribute("ry", minorAxis);
            gcNode.appendChild(ellipseNode);
        }
}
```

The SVG document ArchEllipses1.svg contains a CDATA section with a <script> element, which in turn contains the drawSpiral() function whose main loop renders a set of dynamically created SVG <ellipse> elements. Each SVG <ellipse> element is created in the SVG namespace that is specified in the variable svgNS, after which values are assigned to the required attributes of an ellipse. After each SVG <ellipse> element is dynamically created, the element is appended to the DOM.

CSS3 and SVG

CSS3 selectors can reference SVG documents using the CSS3 url() function, which means that you can incorporate SVG-based graphics effects (including animation) in your HTML pages. The HTML Web page Blue3D-Circle1.html references the CSS stylesheet Blue3DCircle1.css in order to render an SVG circle with styling effects.

CSS3 and SVG Bar Charts

The HTML5 page CSS3SVGBarChart1.html references the CSS3 stylesheet CSS3SVGBarChart1.css and the SVG document CSS3SVG-BarChart1.svg in order to render an SVG circle, a bar chart, and multi-column text.

SIMILARITIES AND DIFFERENCES BETWEEN SVG AND CSS3

This section briefly summarizes the features that are common to SVG and CSS3 and also the features that are unique to each technology.

SVG and CSS3 both provide support for the following:

- Linear and radial gradients
- 2D graphics and animation effects
- Creating shapes such as rectangles, circles, and ellipses
- WAI ARIA

SVG provides support for the following features that are not available in CSS3:

- Bezier curves
- Hierarchical object definitions
- Custom glyphs
- Rendering text along an arbitrary path
- Defining event listeners on SVG objects
- Programmatic creation of 2D shapes using JavaScript
- "Accessibility" to XML-based technologies and tools

CSS3 provides support for the following features that are not available in SVG:

- 3D graphics and animation effects
- Multi-column rendering of text
- WebGL-oriented functionality (e.g., CSS Shaders)

Note that SVG filters and CSS filters will become one and the same at some point in the not-too-distant future.

In general, SVG is better suited than CSS3 for large data sets that will be used for data visualization, and you can reference the SVG document (which might render some type of chart) in a CSS3 selector using the CSS3 url() function. You have already seen such an example in Chapter 3, where the SVG document contains the layout for a bar chart. In general, there might be additional processing involved where data is retrieved or aggregated from one or more sources (such as databases and Web services), and then manipulated using some programming language (such as XSLT, Java, or JavaScript) in order to programmatically create an SVG document or perhaps create SVG elements programmatically in a browser session.

TOOLKITS FOR SVG

There are several excellent toolkits that use SVG, such as Bonsai, D3, and Raphael, whose respective homepages are here:

http://bonsaijs.org/
http://d3js.org/
http://raphaeljs.com/

These toolkits generate SVG code. The following related open source projects contain many code samples:

http://code.google.com/p/bonsai-graphics/ (TBD)
http://code.google.com/p/d3-graphics/
http://code.google.com/p/raphael-graphics/

SUMMARY

This chapter introduced you to SVG and how to create various visual effects using SVG. In particular you learned how to:

- Render basic 2D shapes in SVG
- Use SVG linear and radial gradients
- Render a cube in SVG
- Create Bezier curves
- Create shadow effects
- Use SVG filters
- Render text along a path
- Use SVG transforms
- Use the SVG `scale()` and `translate()` functions
- Use the `rotate()` and `skew()` functions
- Create animation effects in SVG
- Embed JavaScript in SVG
- Combine SVG and CSS3

INTRODUCTION TO HTML5 CANVAS

This chapter provides an overview of HTML5 Canvas, which is a technology that enables you to write graphics programs that draw directly to a part of a Web page. HTML5 Canvas supports various APIs for rendering 2D shapes with an assortment of graphics effects. The first part of this chapter shows you how to render line segments, rectangles, and circles in HTML5 Canvas, and also how to combine HTML5 Canvas with CSS3 stylesheets.

The second part introduces you to linear and radial gradients in HTML5 Canvas, with examples of how to apply them to Bezier curves and JPG files. The third part of this chapter discusses HTML5 Canvas transforms that enable you to scale, translate, rotate, and skew 2D shapes and JPG images. If you want to explore additional HTML5 Canvas graphics after you have finished reading this chapter, an extensive set of code samples is available here:

http://code.google.com/p/html5-canvas-graphics

Keep in mind that it's also important for you to assess the tradeoff (time, effort, and cost) between writing low-level Canvas-based graphics code, such as the code samples in this chapter, versus the availability of open source projects and commercial products.

WHAT IS HTML5 CANVAS?

Several years ago Canvas began in OSX as a widget toolkit. After Canvas had already been available in the Safari browser, it became a specification for the Web, and now it's commonly referred to as HTML5 Canvas.

HTML5 Canvas uses "immediate mode," which is a write-and-forget approach to rendering graphics. Thus, if you want to write a sketching program in HTML5 Canvas and you also want to provide an "undo" feature, then you must programmatically keep track of everything that users have drawn on the screen. On the other hand, SVG uses a "retained mode," which involves a DOM (Document Object Model) structure that keeps track of the rendered objects and their relationship to one another.

A good overview of some features/advantages of HTML5 Canvas here:

http://thinkvitamin.com/code/how-to-draw-with-html-5-canvas/

If you need HTML5 Canvas support in Internet Explorer 8 or earlier, you can use ExplorerCanvas, which is an open source project that is available here:

http://code.google.com/p/explorercanvas/

You can use the preceding code project simply by including the following code snippet in your HTML Web pages:

```
<!-- [if IE < 9]><script src="excanvas.js"></script><![endif]-->
```

One point to consider is when it's advantageous to use HTML5 Canvas instead of a technology such as SVG. A very good article containing examples and diagrams that compares the use of HTML5 Canvas and SVG is here:

http://blogs.msdn.com/b/ie/archive/2011/04/22/thoughts-on-when-to-use-canvas-and-svg.aspx

THE HTML5 CANVAS COORDINATE SYSTEM

In the HTML5 Canvas coordinate system, the origin is the upper-left corner of the screen (not the lower-left corner), and the unit of measurement is the pixel. In addition, the x-axis is horizontal and the positive direction is toward the right. The y-axis is vertical, but the positive direction is *downward*, which is the opposite direction of most graphs in a typical mathematics textbook.

As a simple illustration, Figure 4.1 displays four points in an HTML5 <canvas> element.

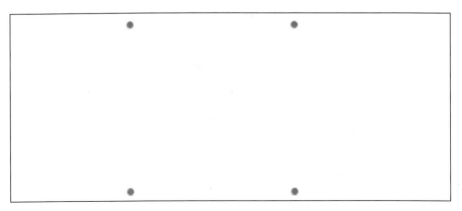

FIGURE 4.1 Four points rendered in HTML5 Canvas

If you start from the origin (the upper-left corner of the screen) and move 50 pixels to the right, followed by 50 pixels downward, you will reach the upper-left point in Figure 4.1. Similar reasoning applies to the other three points with coordinates (150,50), (50,150), and (150,150) in Figure 4.1.

Listing 4.1 displays a minimal HTML5 Web page that is ready for rendering HTML5 Canvas-based graphics, which is the format for the Canvas-based code samples in this chapter. Note that if you launch this code in a browser session, you will only see a blank screen.

LISTING 4.1 Canvas1.html

```
<!DOCTYPE html>
<html lang="en">
 <head>
  <meta charset="utf-8">
  <title>Canvas Drawing Rectangles</title>

  <script><!--
    window.addEventListener('load', function () {
      // Get the canvas element
      var elem = document.getElementById('myCanvas');
      if (!elem || !elem.getContext) {
        return;
      }

      // Get the canvas 2d context
      var context = elem.getContext('2d');
      if (!context) {
        return;
      }

      // Insert your custom Canvas graphics code here
      }, false);
    // --></script>
 </head>

 <body>
  <p>
    <canvas id="myCanvas" width="300" height="300">No support for
Canvas.
    </canvas>
   </p>
  </body>
</html>
```

Listing 4.1 contains an HTML <head> element that checks for the existence of an HTML <canvas> element inside the HTML <body> element of the Web page, and then gets the 2D context from the HTML <canvas> element. If you skip over the various conditional statements in Listing 4.1, there are two lines of code that enable us to get a reference to the variable context, which represents a drawable surface. If you launch Listing 4.1 in a browser that does not support HTML5 Canvas (such as IE 6), the text message "No support for Canvas" is displayed.

The following code snippet is executed whenever you launch the Web page because of an anonymous JavaScript function that is executed during the `load` event:

```
<script><!--
window.addEventListener('load', function () {
  // do something here
}, false);
// --></script>
```

Now that you understand the underlying code for rendering Canvas-based 2D shapes, you can focus on the code that actually draws some 2D shapes, starting with the example in the next section.

LINE SEGMENTS, RECTANGLES, CIRCLES, AND SHADOW EFFECTS

HTML5 Canvas provides the `fillRect()` method for rendering a rectangle, which requires the upper-left vertex (defined by its x-coordinate and its y-coordinate) of the rectangle, the width of the rectangle, and the height of the desired rectangle. Its syntax is shown here:

```
context.fillRect(x, y, width, height);
```

HTML5 Canvas allows you to render line segments by specifying the `(x,y)` coordinates of the two endpoints of a line segment, with the APIs `moveTo()` and `lineTo()` that look like this:

```
context.moveTo(x1, y1);
context.lineTo(x2, y2);
```

You create a shadow effect by assigning values to three shadow-related attributes that control the size of the underlying shadow and also the extent of the "fuzziness" of the shadow, as shown here:

```
context.shadowOffsetX = shadowX;
context.shadowOffsetY = shadowY;
context.shadowBlur    = 4;
```

You can also assign (R,G,B) or (R,G,B,A) values to `shadowColor` (which is an attribute of the drawing context) as shown here:

```
context.shadowColor   = "rgba(0,0,64,1.0)";
```

The portion of the HTML5 Web page `RandRectanglesShadow. html` in Listing 4.2 uses this technique in order to render a set of randomly generated rectangles with a shadow effect.

_____
NOTE The complete listing for this HTML Web page is on the DVD, and it contains the declarations for all the JavaScript variables (which are not shown in Listing 4.2).

LISTING 4.2 RandRectanglesShadow.html

```
<head>
      redrawCanvas = function() {
         // clear the canvas before drawing new set of rectangles
         context.clearRect(0, 0, elem.width, elem.height);

         for(var r=0; r<rectCount; r++) {
            basePointX = canWidth*Math.random();
            basePointY = canHeight*Math.random();

            // Alternate shadow effect based on an even/odd
            // click count with different (R,G,B,A) values
            if(clickCount % 2 == 0) {
               context.shadowColor    = "rgba(0,0,64,1.0)";
            } else {
               context.shadowColor    = "rgba(64,0,0,1.0)";
            }

            // code that specifies the size and also the
         // "fuzziness" of the underlying shadow effect
            context.shadowOffsetX = shadowX;
            context.shadowOffsetY = shadowY;
            context.shadowBlur    = 4;
            context.lineWidth     = 1;

            // render a colored rectangle
            colorIndex = Math.floor(basePointX)%fillStyles.length;
            context.fillStyle = fillStyles[colorIndex];

            context.fillRect(basePointX, basePointY,
                        rectWidth, rectHeight);

            ++clickCount;
         }
      }

      // render a set of random rectangles
      redrawCanvas();
   }, false);
   // --></script>
</head>
```

Listing 4.2 defines the JavaScript function `redrawCanvas()` that contains a loop for rendering the rectangles on the screen. The loop calculates the coordinates of the upper-left vertex of each rectangle as shown here:

```
basePointX = canWidth*Math.random();
basePointY = canHeight*Math.random();
```

The next part of the loop assigns the background color (which alternates between a dark blue and dark red shadow), and then sets up a shadow effect by specifying values for the attributes `shadowOffsetX`, `shadowOffsetY`, and `shadowBlur`. The actual rendering of each rectangle is performed by the method `context.fillRect()`.

Although shadow effects create a pleasing effect, they also have an impact on performance. You can also create a shadow effect for rectangles by first rendering a black rectangle and then rendering a red rectangle on top of the black rectangle, as shown here:

```
// render a black rectangle
context.fillStyle = '#000';
context.fillRect(50+shadowX, 50+shadowY, 200, 100);

// render a red rectangle
context.fillStyle = '#f00';
context.fillRect(50, 50, 200, 100);
```

The values for shadowX and shadowY determine the size of the background "shadow," and the choice of positive versus negative values for shadowX and shadowY will determine the relative position of the black rectangle with respect to the red rectangle.

The CSS stylesheet CSS3Background2.css contains two similar CSS3 selectors for rendering the HTML5 <canvas> element defined in Listing 4.2, also a hover-based selector that changes the background of the HTML5 <canvas> element whenever users hover over this element with their mouse. The #myCanvas selector defines a radial gradient, followed by two repeating radial gradients that specify various combinations of red, green, yellow, and blue at different pixel locations. A key point involves the use of transparent, which changes the gap between consecutive colors that are rendered.

As you can see in the definition of the #myCanvas selector, there are many possible combinations available for the colors, the gradients (and their types), and the colors for the gradients, along with the values for the background-size attribute. There is no "right" way to define these patterns; feel free to experiment with different combinations, and you might create unexpectedly pleasing results.

Figure 4.2 displays a set of randomly generated rectangles with a shadow effect based on RandRectanglesShadow.html in Listing 4.2, rendered in landscape mode on an Asus Prime tablet with Android ICS.

HTML5 CANVAS LINEAR GRADIENTS

HTML5 Canvas provides two primary types of color gradients (similar to SVG and CSS3): *linear gradients* and *radial gradients.*

Linear color gradients can be further sub-divided into three types: horizontal linear gradients, vertical linear gradients, and diagonal linear gradients. Thus, HTML5 Canvas provides color gradients that enable you to create pleasing visual effects.

A linear gradient is defined in terms of addColorStop elements, each of which contains a decimal (between 0 and 1) and a hexadecimal value that represents a color. For example, if you define a linear gradient with an initial color of #FF0000 (the hexadecimal value for red) and a final color of

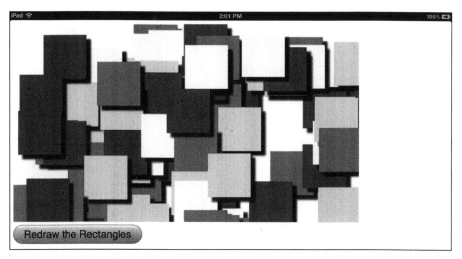

FIGURE 4.2 Canvas random rectangles on an Asus Prime tablet with Android ICS

#000000 (the hexadecimal value for black), then the resultant color gradient will range (in a linear fashion) from red to black. Linear gradients enable you to create vivid and interesting color combinations, and they are available in three varieties: horizontal, vertical, and diagonal. "Linear gradient" and "linear color gradient" are used interchangeably in this book.

Horizontal, Vertical, and Diagonal Linear Gradients

As you learned in the introduction of this chapter, HTML5 Canvas supports the method createLinearGradient() that you can use to programmatically create linear gradients, and its syntax looks like this:

```
context.createLinearGradient(startX, startY, endX, endY);
```

The HTML5 page LGradRectangles1.html in Listing 4.3 demonstrates how to render a set of rectangles with horizontal, vertical, and diagonal linear gradients. Listing 4.3 references the CSS3 stylesheet HoverAnimation1.css that applies CSS3 keyframes-based 2D animation to the first HTML5 <canvas> element whenever users hover over this <canvas> element with their mouse. Listing 4.3 also references the CSS3 stylesheet HoverAnimation2.css, which acts in a similar fashion; however, this stylesheet applies CSS3 3D animation effects to the second HTML5 <canvas> element in Listing 4.3. Since the animation techniques in these CSS stylesheets are discussed in Chapter 2, we will omit them from this chapter, but the entire source code is available on the DVD.

LISTING 4.3 LGradRectangles1.html

```
<!DOCTYPE html>
<html lang="en">
  <head>
```

```
<meta charset="utf-8">
<title>Linear Gradient Rectangles</title>

<link href="HoverAnimation1.css" rel="stylesheet" type="text/css">
   <link href="HoverAnimation2.css" rel="stylesheet" type="text/
css">

<script><!--
   window.addEventListener('load', function () {

      // code omitted for brevity

      redrawCanvas = function() {
         // upper left rectangle: horizontal linear gradient
         currentX = basePointX;
         currentY = basePointY;

         gradient1 = context.createLinearGradient(
                                 currentX,
                                 currentY,
                                 currentX+rectWidth,
                                 currentY+0*rectHeight);

         gradient1.addColorStop(0, '#f00');
         gradient1.addColorStop(1, '#00f');
         context.fillStyle = gradient1;
         context.fillRect(currentX, currentY,
                       rectWidth, rectHeight);

         // the following code is omitted for brevity:
         // upper right rectangle: vertical linear gradient
        // render the lower rectangles in the second <canvas> element
         // lower left rectangle: diagonal linear gradient
         // lower right rectangle: diagonal linear gradient
      }

      // render linear gradient rectangles
      redrawCanvas();
   }, false);
   // --></script>
 </head>
</body>
</html>
```

Listing 4.3 renders four rectangles with linear gradient shading. The linear gradients have two, three, or four invocations of the addColor-Stop() method, using various combinations of colors (expressed in hexadecimal form) so that you can see some of the gradient effects that are possible.

Experiment with different values for the color stop definitions to see how their values change the appearance of the rendered rectangles.

Figure 4.3 displays a set of randomly generated rectangles with a shadow effect based on LGradRectangles1.html in Listing 4.4, in landscape mode on a Nexus 7 tablet with Android JellyBean.

RADIAL COLOR GRADIENTS

A radial color gradient is the second type of HTML5 Canvas-based color gradient. You can define a radial color gradient via the `createRadialGradient()` method, using the `addColorStop()` method to add color values. Its syntax (without the `addColorStop()` method) looks like this:

```
context.createRadialGradient(startCent
erX, startCenterY, startRadius,
    endsCenterX, endCenterY, endRadius);
```

A *radial* color gradient can be compared to the ripple effect that is created when you drop a stone in a pond, where each "ripple" has a color that changes in a gradient fashion. Each ripple corresponds to a color stop element. For example, if you define a radial gradient with a start color of `#FF0000` (which is red)

FIGURE 4.3 Linear gradient rectangles on a Nexus 7 tablet with Android JellyBean

and an end color of `#000000` (which is black), then the resultant color gradient will range—in a radial fashion—from red to black. Radial gradients can also contain multiple start/stop color combinations. The point to keep in mind is that radial gradients change colors in a *linear* fashion, but the rendered colors are drawn in an expanding *radial* fashion. Note that "radial gradient" and "radial color gradient" are used interchangeably in this book.

Listing 4.4 displays the abbreviated contents of `RGradRectangles1.html` that renders line segments, rectangles, and circles in an HTML5 `<canvas>` element using linear and radial gradients.

LISTING 4.4 RGradRectangles1.html

```
<!DOCTYPE html>
<html lang="en">
<head>
 <meta charset="utf-8">
 <title>Radial Gradient Rectangles</title>

 <script><!--
    window.addEventListener('load', function () {
       redrawCanvas = function() {
          // upper left rectangle
          currentX = basePointX;
          currentY = basePointY;

          gradient1 = context.createRadialGradient(currentX,
                                                    currentY,
                                                    0,
                                                    currentX+rectWidth,
                                                    currentY+rectHeight,
```

```
                                                    rectWidth);

          gradient1.addColorStop(0, '#f00');
          gradient1.addColorStop(1, '#00f');
          context.fillStyle = gradient1;
          context.fillRect(currentX, currentY,
                           rectWidth, rectHeight);

          // upper right rectangle
          // lower left rectangle
          // lower right rectangle
      }
      // render a set of rectangles
      redrawCanvas();
    }, false);
    // --></script>
  </head>
</html>
```

Listing 4.4 is similar to Listing 4.3, except for the use of a radial gradient (instead of a linear gradient) that ranges in a radial fashion from blue to red. The method addColorStop() is invoked four times in order to add four "color stop values" to the radial gradient. Listing 4.4 also references HoverAnimation1.css that whose entire source code is available on the DVD.

Figure 4.4 displays a set of rectangles with a radial gradient based on RGradRectangles1.html in Listing 4.5, in landscape mode on an iPad 3.

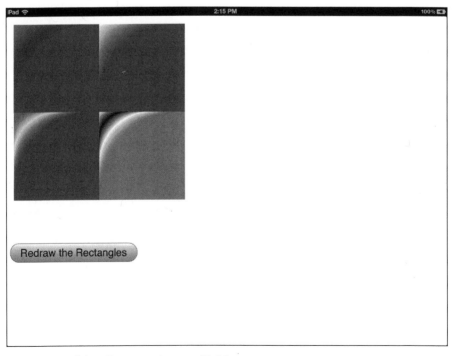

FIGURE 4.4 Radial gradient rectangles on an iPad 3

BEZIER CURVES

HTML5 Canvas provides support for both quadratic Bezier curves and cubic Bezier curves. Cubic Bezier curves have two end points and two control points, whereas quadratic Bezier curves have two end points and a single control point. The x-coordinate and y-coordinate of a cubic Bezier curve can be represented as a parameterized cubic equation whose coefficients are derived from the control points and the end points.

The syntax for the HTML5 Canvas `quadraticCurveTo()` method looks like this:

```
quadraticCurveTo(controlX, controlY, endX, endY);
```

The syntax for the HTML5 Canvas `bezierCurveTo()` method looks like this:

```
bezierCurveTo(controlX1,controlY1,controlX2,controlY2,endX,endY);
```

The HTML5 page `LRGradQCBezier1.html` references the CSS stylesheets `CSS3Background6.css` and `HoverAnimation1.css` (these files are on the DVD) and also renders a quadratic Bezier curve with linear gradient shading and a cubic Bezier curve with radial gradient shading.

As an exercise, modify the code in `LRGradQCBezier1.html` to render a small circle at the location of the control points and the endpoints by using the HTML5 Canvas `arc()` method that is used in order to render a pie chart in the HTML Web page `PieChart1.html` on the DVD. You can use the `arc()` method to render a circle by means of the following syntax:

```
context.arc(xCoord, yCoord, radius, 0, 360, 0);
```

Figure 4.5 renders the quadratic and cubic Bezier curves that are defined in the HTML5 Web page `LRGradQCBezier1.html` in landscape mode on an iPad 3.

RENDERING IMAGES ON CANVAS WITH CSS3 SELECTORS

HTML5 Canvas supports the rendering of JPG files, and you can also apply CSS selectors to the HTML5 `<canvas>` element. Listing 4.5 displays the contents of `Image1.html`, and `Image1.css` defines selectors that match elements in Listing 5.6.

LISTING 4.5 Image1.html

```
<!DOCTYPE html>
<html lang="en">
<head>
<head>
 <meta charset="utf-8">
 <title>Images and CSS3 Selectors</title>
```

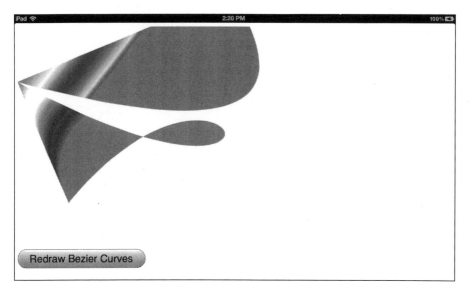

FIGURE 4.5 Gradient Bezier curves on an iPad 3

```html
<link href="Image1.css" rel="stylesheet" type="text/css">
<link href="HoverAnimation1.css" rel="stylesheet" type="text/css">

<script>
  function renderJPG() {
     // Create a radial gradient:
     var rGradient = context.createRadialGradient(
                            basePointX+rectWidth/2,
                            basePointY+rectWidth/2,
                            gradientR,
                            basePointX+rectWidth/2,
                            basePointY+rectWidth/2,
                            3*gradientR);

     rGradient.addColorStop(0,   '#FF0000');
     rGradient.addColorStop(0.5, '#FFFF00');
     rGradient.addColorStop(1,   '#000044');

     // rectangular background with radial gradient:
     context.fillStyle = rGradient;
     context.fillRect(basePointX-offsetX,
                 basePointY-offsetY,
                 rectWidth+borderX+2*offsetX,
                 rectHeight+borderY+2*offsetY);

     // Load the JPG
     var myImage = new Image();
     myImage.onload = function() {
        context.drawImage(myImage,
                       basePointX,
                       basePointY,
                       rectWidth,
                       rectHeight);
```

```
        }

            myImage.src = "Laurie1.jpeg";
        }
    </script>
</head>
</html>
```

Listing 4.5 contains JavaScript code that creates a radial gradient `rGra-dient` with three color stops. Next, a rectangle is rendered with using the radial gradient that is referenced by the variable `rGradient`, followed by a section of code that renders the JPG file `Laurie1.jpeg`. The inline CSS code in the `<style>` element renders a white background with a zero-width border (so it's invisible), but you can modify this CSS code to produce additional effects. The `<body>` element contains the `onload` attribute whose value is `renderJPG()`, which is a JavaScript function that renders the JPG file inside the HTML5 `<canvas>` element.

Incidentally, HTML5 Canvas also supports a `clip()` method that enables you to "crop" JPG files in various ways. Moreover, you can perform compositing effects, and you can even manipulate the individual pixels of a JPG file. Search the Internet for articles that describe the technical details of these effects.

Figure 4.6 displays a JPG file with two radial gradient background effects, in landscape mode taken on a Nexus 7 tablet with Android JellyBean.

HTML5 Canvas also provides the method `createPattern(image, type)` that enables you to render a set of images according to a `pattern` type, whose values can be `repeat`, `repeat-x`, `repeat-y`, and `no-re-peat`. An example of the syntax (and also how to use it) looks like this:

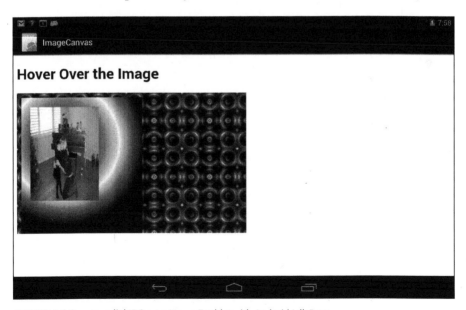

FIGURE 4.6 Canvas radial JPG on a Nexus 7 tablet with Android JellyBean

```
var pattern = canvas.createPattern(img,"repeat");
canvas.fillStyle = pattern;
canvas.fillRect(0,0,500,300);
```

Listing 4.6 displays the contents of `RepeatingImage1.html` that illustrates how to repeat a JPG image on an HTML5 `<canvas>` element.

LISTING 4.6 RepeatingImage1.html

```
function modImage(e) {
   img = e.target;
   var pattern = canvas.createPattern(img,"repeat");

   canvas.fillStyle = pattern;
   canvas.fillRect(0,0,500,300);
}
```

Listing 4.6 contains the following line of code that invokes the JavaScript `init()` method when this Web page is loaded into a browser:
`window.addEventListener("load", init, false);`

The `init()` method finds an HTML5 `<canvas>` element in the Web page, and for simplicity, no error checking is performed (which can be handled by using code from previous examples). The `init()` method also initializes a JavaScript variable `img` that references a JPG file, and then adds an event listener that executes the JavaScript function `modImage()`.

Finally, the `modImage()` method invokes the Canvas method `createPattern()` with the parameter repeat in order to create a rectangular grid of images that is based on one PNG file (which is `BlueBall1.png` in this example).

Figure 4.7 displays `RepeatingImage1.html` in Listing 4.6 in landscape mode on a Chrome browser on a Macbook.

HTML5 CANVAS TRANSFORMS

HTML5 Canvas enables you to rotate, scale, shear, or translate (which shifts horizontally and/or vertically) 2D shapes and text strings with the following methods:

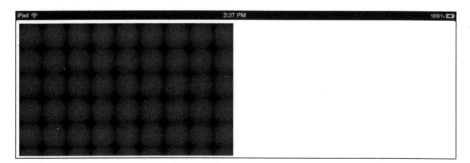

FIGURE 4.7 Repeating JPG on a Chrome browser on a Macbook

```
rotate(x,y)
scale(x,y)
transform(x1,y1,x2,y2,x3,y3)
translate(x,y)
```

One thing to keep in mind is that you specify the transforms that you want to apply (along with setting attributes values) before actually rendering a graphics shape in your HTML5 Web pages.

The following code snippets illustrate sample values that you can use in the preceding Canvas methods, where `context` is a JavaScript variable that references the context of an HTML5 `<canvas>` element:

```
context.rotate(30*Math.PI/180);
context.scale(0.8, 0.4);
context.translate(100, 200);
context.transform(1, 0, 0.5, 1, 0, 0);
```

The `rotate()` method in the preceding code block references the Java-Script constant `Math.PI` whose value equals `PI` radians. In case you have forgotten, `PI` radians equal 180 degrees, so `2*PI` radians is 360 degrees, and `PI/2` radians is 90 degrees. Hence, `Math.PI/6` radians (or `30*Math.PI/180`) is the same as 30 degrees. You won't need to know anything more about radians, but feel free to perform an Internet search if you want to read some tutorials that provide additional examples.

Two additional APIs in HTML5 Canvas are `save()` and `restore()`, which enable you to save the current state of a canvas state, make some changes, and then restore the original state of the canvas. You can save (and later restore) a canvas state after having applied any of the transformations listed in this section, and also after having specified values for shadow-related attributes (among others). You can invoke the `save()` and `restore()` methods multiple times on a canvas state, which makes these two methods very useful for game-related Web pages.

Listing 4.7 displays the contents of `CanvasTransforms1.html` that illustrates how to apply four HTML5 Canvas transforms to a text string.

LISTING 4.7 *CanvasTransforms1.html*

```
<!DOCTYPE html>
<html lang="en">
 <head>
 <meta charset="utf-8">
 <title>Linear Gradient Rectangles</title>

  <script><!--
    window.addEventListener('load', function () {
      redrawCanvas = function() {
        // render text...
        context.fillStyle   = "#f00";
        context.strokeStyle = "#00f"
        context.fillText("Hello World", 40, 150);
        context.fill();

        // render scaled text...
```

```
            context.scale(0.3, 0.3);
            context.fillStyle    = "#ff0";
            context.fillText("Hello World", 40, 100);
            context.fill();

            // render skewed text...
        context.transform(1, 10*Math.PI/180, 20*Math.PI/180, 1,0,0);
            context.fillStyle    = "#0f0";
            context.fillText("Hello World", 0, 700);
            context.fill();

            // render rotated text...
            context.transform(1, -10*Math.PI/180, -20*Math.PI/180,
1,0,0);
            context.rotate(-Math.PI/8);
            context.scale(3, 1);

            context.fillStyle    = "#00f";
            context.fillText("Hello World", 0, 1400);
            context.fill();
        }

    redrawCanvas();
    }, false);
    // --></script>
  </head>
```

Listing 4.7 contains the usual initialization code that you've seen in the other examples in this chapter, and the attributes for rendering the text strings are set in this code block:

```
context.shadowColor    = "rgba(0,0,128,0.5)";
context.shadowOffsetX = 5;
context.shadowOffsetY = 5;
context.shadowBlur     = 10;
context.lineWidth      = 2;
context.font           = "Bold 60pt Helvetica";
```

You have already seen examples of the first five attributes, and as you would expect, the `font` attribute enables you to set the font family and the font size.

The `redraw()` JavaScript function renders the string "Hello World," and then three more times after applying a transform to this text string.

Figure 4.8 displays the result of rendering `CanvasTransforms1.html` in Listing 4.7, which displays four text strings in a landscape-mode screenshot on an iPad 3.

Experiment with the transformations in this section by applying them to 2D shapes from earlier code samples in this chapter.

ADDITIONAL CODE SAMPLES

The HTML page `BarChart2LG1.html` references `CSS32Background2.css` in order to render a bar chart with linear gradient shading. The HTML Web page contains one loop for initializing the randomly gener-

FIGURE 4.8 Rendering text with transforms on an iPad 3

ated heights of the bar chart elements, followed by another loop that renders those bar chart elements with a linear gradient consisting of four color stops.

The HTML page `BarChart13D1Mouse.html` renders a mouse-enabled bar chart with a three-dimensional effect. In HTML5 Canvas, you can render a 3D bar chart by rendering the top face (a parallelogram), the front face (a rectangle), and the right face (a parallelogram) of the cube for each "bar element" in the bar chart.

The HTML5 page `PieChart1.html` renders a pie chart by initializing an array of values for a set of angles (measured in degrees), followed by a block of code that uses the HTML5 Canvas `arc()` method with the values in the `wedgeAngles` array in order to render the pie chart. Note that the angle span of the "wedges" changes in a random fashion whenever users reload this HTML Web page.

OTHER HTML5 CANVAS TOOLKITS

There are several very good JavaScript toolkits available that provide a later of abstraction on top of HTML5 Canvas, including `Easel.js`, `Fabric.js`, `jCanvaScript.js`, and `Paper.js`. In addition to the code samples that are available on the respective homepage of these toolkits, additional `Easel.js` code samples are here:

http://code.google.com/p/easeljs-graphics
http://code.google.com/p/fabricjs-graphics/
http://code.google.com/p/jcanvascript-graphics/
http://code.google.com/p/paperjs-graphics/

SUMMARY

This chapter introduced you to HTML5 Canvas and showed you examples of creating 2D shapes with the HTML5 `<canvas>` element. You also learned how to manipulate HTML5 Web pages with Canvas-based 2D shapes. In particular, you learned how to do the following in HTML5 Canvas:

- Render line segments, rectangles, and circles
- Create linear and radial gradients
- Create Bezier curves
- Display JPG files

MEDIA AND HARDWARE SUPPORT HTML5

This chapter starts with a discussion of the new HTML5 `<audio>` and `<video>` elements for playing audio and video clips. Next you'll learn about the Web Audio APIs, along with a code sample that illustrates how to convert an audio file into a graphical representation using the HTML5 `<canvas>` element. The final portion of this chapter delves into some hardware-related APIs, including accelerometer and battery, with code samples that illustrate how to use them.

THE HTML5 <AUDIO> ELEMENT

The HTML5 `<audio>` tag is very simple to use, and its syntax looks like this:

```
<audio src="Sample1.mp3" controls autoplay loop>
  HTML5 audio tag not supported
</audio>
```

The HTML5 `<audio>` tag supports several attributes, including `auto-play` (play the audio as soon as it's ready), `controls` (displays the `play`, `pause`, and except for Chrome, the `volume` controls), `loop` (replays the audio), `preload` (loads the audio so it's ready to run on page load), and `src` (specifies the location of the audio file).

A minimalistic example of how to use the `<audio>` tag in an HTML5 Web page is illustrated in Listing 5.1, which displays the contents of `HTML5Au-dio1.html`.

LISTING 5.1 HTML5Audio1.html

```
<!doctype html>
<html>
<head>
  <meta charset="utf-8" />
```

```
  <title>HTML5 Audio</title>
</head>

<body>
  <h1>Audio Recording in Japanese</h1>

  <!-- Display control buttons -->
  <audio src="Japanese1.mp3" controls autoplay loop>
     HTML5 audio tag not supported  </audio>
 </body>
</html>
```

Listing 5.1 is very straightforward: boilerplate code and one HTML5 <audio> element that specifies the mp3 audio file Japanese1.mp3, along with audio controls that enable users to replay the audio clip.

Different browsers support different audio file formats; fortunately, the HTML5 <audio> tag supports a <source> element, which in turn provides an src attribute that enables you to specify different file formats, as shown here:

```
<audio controls="true">
   <source src="s.mp3" type="audio/mp3">
   <source src="s.ogg" type="audio/ogg">
   <source src="s.aac" type="audio/mp4">
   HTML5 audio not supported
</audio>
```

The preceding HTML5 <audio> tag specifies a file in multiple formats. When you launch a Web page with this tag, your browser will start from the first <source> element in order to find a format that it recognizes and then play the audio file that is specified in the src attribute.

In addition, you can also programmatically control the <audio> tag using JavaScript code. Listing 5.2 displays the contents of an HTML5 Web page with an <audio> tag and some error-handling JavaScript code.

LISTING 5.2 HTML5Audio2.html

```
<!DOCTYPE HTML>
<html lang="en">
 <head>
  <meta charset="utf-8" />
  <title>HTML5 Audio With Error Detection</title>

  <script>
   function ReportError(e) {
    switch (e.target.error.code) {
      case e.target.error.MEDIA_ERR_ABORTED:
        alert("User aborted the playback.");
        break;
      case e.target.error.MEDIA_ERR_NETWORK:
        alert("Network error.");
        break;
      case e.target.error.MEDIA_ERR_DECODE:
        alert("The File is Corrupted.");
        break;
```

```
     case e.target.error.MEDIA_ERR_SRC_NOT_SUPPORTED:
       alert("Unsupported Format or File not Found.");
       break;
     default:
       alert("An Unknown Error Occurred.");
       break;
   }
 }
</script>
</head>

<body>
 <h1>HTML 5 Audio</h1>
 <audio controls onerror="ReportError(event)" src="Japanese1.mp3">
 </audio>
</body>
</html>
```

Listing 5.2 contains the JavaScript function `ReportError()` that is invoked when an error occurs while playing the audio file in this `<audio>` element:

```
<audio controls onerror="ReportError(event)" src="Japanese1.mp3">
```

The `ReportError()` function contains a `switch` statement that displays an alert when any of the following errors occurs:

```
MEDIA_ERR_ABORTED
MEDIA_ERR_NETWORK
MEDIA_ERR_DECODE
MEDIA_ERR_SRC_NOT_SUPPORTED
```

Some interesting audio demos in Google Chrome are here:

http://chromium.googlecode.com/svn/trunk/samples/audio/index.html

If you want to learn more about HTML5 Audio features, you can read the W3C Audio specification here:

https://dvcs.w3.org/hg/audio/raw-file/tip/webaudio/specification.html

The HTML5 <Video> Element

The HTML5 `<video>` tag can be as minimal as the HTML5 `<audio>` tag, and its syntax looks like this:

```
<video>
  <source type="video/mp4" src="filename">
</video>
```

As you might have surmised, you can also include multiple `<source>` elements in the HTML5 `<video>` element, as shown here:

```
<video poster="MyVideo.gif" controls>
  <source src='MyVideo.mp4'
          type='video/mp4; codecs="avc1.4D401E, mp4a.40.2"'>
  <source src='MyVideo.ogv'
          type='video/ogg; codecs="theora, vorbis"'>
```

```
<source src='MyVideo.webm'
        type='video/webm; codecs="vp8.0, vorbis"'>
<p>Your browser does not support the video element</p>
</video>
```

The current HTML5 specification does not specify any video formats whose support is required, but the following video formats are commonly supported in modern browsers:

- MP4 (MPEG4 files with H.264 video codec and AAC audio codec)
- Ogg (Ogg files with Theodora video codec and Vorbis audio codec) are commonly supported in modern browsers. On mobile devices, the iPhone simulator supports MP4, Android hardware support h.264, and the Android simulator supports Ogg Vorbis.
- WebM or VP8, which is a royalty-free open audio-video compression format with the .WebM extension (currently has a low adoption rate)

On the mobile side of things, both iOS and Android only support MP4 video (but according to one unconfirmed report, Android 4.1 will support WebM).

Listing 5.3 displays the contents of `HTML5Video1.html` that illustrates how to play a video file in an HTML5 Web page.

LISTING 5.3 HTML5Video1.html

```
<!DOCTYPE HTML>
<html>
<head>
  <meta charset="utf-8" />
  <title>Working With HTML5 Video</title>
</head>

<body>
  <video width="800" height="500"
         controls poster="Laurie2.jpeg" id="video1">
    <source src="Rectangle1.mov" type="video/mp4">
    <source src="Rectangle1.ogg" type="video/ogg">
  </video>
</body>
</html>
```

Listing 5.3 contains some boilerplate code, along with an HTML5 <video> element whose attributes are similar to the HTML5 <audio> element. Note that the HTML5 <video> element in Listing 5.3 specifies two <source> elements whose src attribute references the same video file, but in two different formats. Browsers handle an HTML5 <video> element in a similar fashion as an HTML5 <audio> element: when you launch an HTML5 Web page with an HTML5 <video> element in a browser, your browser will play the first video whose format is recognized by the browser.

NOTE   You need to provide a video file for Listing 5.3 in order to see the video functionality.

In a previous section, you saw how to use JavaScript to bind to audio elements, and you can do the same thing with video elements (and also include a custom progress bar).

Listing 5.4 displays the contents of HTML5Video2.html that illustrates how to play a video file in an HTML5 Web page that contains error-handling code in JavaScript.

LISTING 5.4 HTML5Video2.html

```
<!DOCTYPE HTML>
<html lang="en">
<head>
  <meta charset="utf-8" />
  <title></title>

  <style>
    /* selectors for playing and paused */
    .paused  { }
    .playing { }
  </style>

  <script>
    function init() {
      var video = document.getElementById("video1");
      var toggle = document.getElementById("toggle1");

      toggle.onclick = function() {
        if (video.paused) {
          video.play();
          toggle.className="playing"
        } else {
          video.pause();
          toggle.className="paused"
        }
      }
    }
  </script>
</head>

<body onload="init()">
  <figure>
    <video src="media/video1.webm" controls autoplay
           id="video1" width="400" height="300"
           data-description="Sample Video">
      This browser does not support the video tag </video>
    <legend>Sample Video</legend>
  </figure>

  <div id="toggle1"> </div>
</body>
</html>
```

Listing 5.4 contains a JavaScript init() method that is executed when the Web page is loaded into a browser, and this method contains JavaScript code that handles the play and pause events for the video element, as shown here:

```
var video = document.getElementById("video1");
var toggle = document.getElementById("toggle1");

toggle.onclick = function() {
   if (video.paused) {
     video.play();
     toggle.className="playing"
   } else {
     video.pause();
     toggle.className="paused"
   }
}
```

Listing 5.4 also contains boilerplate code and an HTML5 <video> element that specifies a video file and also video controls that users can use to control the video, as shown here:

```
<video src="media/video1.webm" controls autoplay
       id="video1" width="400" height="300"
       data-description="Sample Video">
   This browser does not support the video tag
</video>
```

As you can see, the CSS selectors playing and paused are currently empty; their contents would contain properties that perform your styling effects.

——— You need to provide a video file for Listing 5.4 in order to see the video
NOTE functionality.

A useful link with information about the status of HTML5 video and a link to an interesting Web site for HTML5 video support are here:

http://www.longtailvideo.com/html5/
http://videojs.com/

The HTML <video> element also supports the canPlayType() method that enables you to determine programmatically how likely your browser can play different video types. This method returns "probably," "maybe," or an empty string.

Listing 5.5 displays the contents of HTML5Video3.html that illustrates how to check browser support for different video types.

LISTING 5.5 HTML5Video3.html

```
<!DOCTYPE HTML>
<html lang="en">
<head>
  <meta charset="utf-8" />
  <title>Detecting Video Support</title>

  <script>
  var videoTypes = ['video/ogg; codecs="theora, vorbis"',
                    'video/ogg',
```

```
                  'video/mp4',
                  'video/ogv',
                  'video/webm'
                  ];

   function init() {
     var video = document.getElementById("video1");
     var canPlay, videoType;

     for(var v=0; v<videoTypes.length; v++) {
        videoType = videoTypes[v];
        canPlay = video.canPlayType(videoType);

console.log("Type: "+videoType+" Can Play: "+canPlay);
     }
   }
   </script>
</head>

<body onload="init()">
 <figure>
   <video src="media/HelloWorld.ogg" controls autoplay
          id="video1" width="400" height="300"
          data-description="Sample Video">
     This browser does not support the video tag </video>
   <legend>Sample Video</legend>
 </figure>
</body>
</html>
```

Listing 5.5 contains a JavaScript array videoTypes that specifies information about various video formats, and the first entry is the most detailed information. The JavaScript function init() is invoked when the Web page is loaded into a browser, and it contains a loop that iterates through the array of video formats and checks which ones are supported by your browser.

If you launch a Chrome browser (version 19) on a Macbook, you will see the following output in the console:

```
Type: video/ogg; codecs="theora, vorbis" Can Play: probably
Type: video/ogg Can Play: maybe
Type: video/mp4 Can Play: maybe
Type: video/ogv Can Play:
Type: video/webm Can Play: maybe
```

Notice that the first line specifies the codecs. The browser has determined that it can probably play the given video type, whereas the second line is "maybe" because the codecs are not specified.

Popcorn.js: HTML5 Media Framework

Popcorn.js is part of the Mozilla Popcorn project. It's a JavaScript-based HTML5 media framework for creating time-based interactive media. The Popcorn.js homepage and the download link are here:

http://popcornjs.org
http://popcornjs.org/download

Popcorn.js consists of a core JavaScript library (available as a separate download) and plugins. You can also create a customized download of Popcorn.js, along with minified and debug versions. Navigate to the home page for additional information, as well as documentation and a video with a demonstration of Popcorn.js.

HTML5 <Video> and Web Camera Support

You can use the HTML5 `<video>` tag for real-time camera support. This functionality is already available in Opera (see the link below). As this book goes to print, this functionality is available in the `WebKit` "nightly" builds, which is accessible via the `getUserMedia()` API (provided that you specify browser prefixes).

For other useful information regarding HTML5 video, visit this Web site:

http://html5video.org/

Listing 5.6 displays the contents of `WebCamera1.html` that illustrates how to activate a camera in a browser (as of mid-2012 this feature works only in Opera).

LISTING 5.6: WebCamera1.html

```
<!DOCTYPE HTML>
<html>
<head>
  <meta charset="utf-8" />
  <title>HTML5 Web Camera</title>
</head>

<body>
<h1>Web camera display demo</h1>
<video autoplay></video>
<script>
 var video = document.getElementsByTagName('video')[0],
     heading = document.getElementsByTagName('h1')[0];

if(navigator.getUserMedia) {
  navigator.getUserMedia('video', successCallback, errorCallback);
  function successCallback( stream ) {
    video.src = stream;
  }
  function errorCallback( error ) {
    heading.textContent =
        "An error occurred: [CODE " + error.code + "]";
  }
} else {
  heading.textContent =
     "Native Web camera streaming is not supported in this browser";
}
</script>
```

```
</body>
</html>
```

Listing 5.6 checks for the presence of `navigator.getUserMedia`, and if it does exist, then an invocation of the `getUserMedia()` method searches for the HTML5 `<video>` tag and provides both success and failure JavaScript callback functions, as shown here:

```
navigator.getUserMedia('video', successCallback, errorCallback);
```

An Opera build that provides Web camera support for Linux, Mac, Windows, and Android is available for download here:

http://dev.opera.com/articles/view/labs-more-fun-using-the-web-with-getusermedia-and-native-pages/

Although the HTML5 technologies Navigation Timing, RDFa, and Selectors have CR status, they are not discussed in this book.

BATTERY API

The Battery API, which provides information about the battery status of the hosting device, is maintained by the DAP (Device APIs) working group and is in Candidate Recommendation (CR) status. The following simple code snippet writes the battery level to the console each time the level changes:

```
navigator.battery.onlevelchange = function () {
  console.log(navigator.battery.level);
};
```

Listing 5.7 displays the contents of the HTML Web page `Battery.html` that illustrates how to use the Battery API in a Web page.

LISTING 5.7 Battery.html

```
<!DOCTYPE html>
<html>
<head>
  <meta charset="utf-8" />
  <title>Battery Status API Example</title>

 <script>
  var battery = navigator.battery;

  if(battery != null) {
      battery.onchargingchange = function () {
        document.querySelector('#charging').textContent =
          battery.charging ? 'charging' : 'not charging';
        };

      battery.onlevelchange = function () {
          document.querySelector('#level').textContent =
                                      battery.level;
```

```
        };

        battery.ondischargingtimechange = function () {
          document.querySelector('#dischargingTime').textContent =
                                      battery.dischargingTime / 60;
        };
      } else {
        console.log("Battery not Supported in this Browser");
      }
    </script>
  </head>

  <body>
    <div id="charging">(charging state unknown)</div>
    <div id="level">(battery level unknown)</div>
    <div id="dischargingTime">(discharging time unknown)</div>
  </body>
  </html>
```

Listing 5.7 contains JavaScript code that first ensures that `navigator.battery` is non-null, and then defines three straightforward JavaScript functions that handle change-related battery events: `onchargingchange`, `onlevelchange`, and `ondischargingtimechange`. The JavaScript functions simply update the contents of an associated `<div>` element that is located in the `<body>` element of Listing 5.1.

You can find additional information about the Battery API in the W3C specification:

http://www.w3.org/TR/battery-status

VIBRATION API (DAP)

The Vibration API (also maintained by the DAP working group) defines an API that provides access to the vibration mechanism of a hosting device. The Vibration API consists of a single method `vibrate()` whose implementation must run the algorithm for processing vibration patterns (see link below for details).

In the following example the device vibrates for 1 second:

```
// vibrate for 1 second
navigator.vibrate(1000);
```

Using the following code snippet to cause a device to vibrate for 1 second, stop vibration for 0.5 seconds, and vibrate again for 2 seconds:

```
navigator.vibrate([1000, 500, 2000]);
```

Cancel any existing vibrations:

```
navigator.vibrate(0);
```

Cancel any existing vibrations:

```
navigator.vibrate([]);
```

For additional information, navigate to the W3C Vibration API (currently a working draft):

http://www.w3.org/TR/vibration/

HTML5 APIS IN W3C WORKING DRAFT STATUS (WD)

The HTML5 technologies in this section (listed in alphabetical order) currently have a Working Draft status. IndexedDB has WD status and it is discussed in Chapter 1, so we will not repeat that content here. In addition, the following HTML5 technologies also have WD status but they are not discussed in this chapter:

- Media Capture
- RDFa
- Touch Events

AUDIO PROCESSING

The W3C Audio Processing API introduces two APIs: Google's Web Audio API specification and Mozilla's MediaStream Processing API specification. The code sample in this section illustrates how to use the audio APIs for Mozilla, which means that you need to launch the HTML Web page in Firefox.

In Chapter 1, you saw an example of the HTML5 <audio> element, and in this section you will see a code sample that uses the Web Audio APIs, which enable you to access low-level data. The code sample shows you how to play an audio file and then render a set of rectangles that are rendered along a sine wave that represents the amplitude of the sounds in the audio file.

The code sample in this section works in Firefox and Safari 6, and undoubtedly will be available in Chrome in the future. This code sample in Listing 5.11 is one of the few code samples in this book that are not WebKit-based; they are included because they create interesting visual effects.

Listing 5.8 displays the contents of the HTML Web page WebAudio1. html that illustrates how to use the Web Audio API in an HTML Web page.

LISTING 5.8 WebAudio1.html

```
<!DOCTYPE html>
<html lang="en">
<head>
  <meta charset="utf-8" />
  <title>HTML5 Audio Visualization</title>
</head>

<body>
  <h2>Audio Sampling Example</h2>
  <audio tabloop="0" src="HelloWorld.ogg" controls="controls">
  </audio>
  <div>
```

```
<canvas width="512" height="200" style="background-color:yellow;">
  </canvas>

<canvas width="512" height="200" style="background-color:yellow;">
  </canvas>

<canvas width="512" height="200" style="background-color:yellow;">
  </canvas>

<canvas width="512" height="200" style="background-color:yellow;">
  </canvas>
  </div>

<script>
  var sampleCount = 512, rectWidth=sampleCount, rectHeight=200;
  var barWidth = 10, barHeight = 0, deltaX1 = 2, deltaX4 = 5;
  var x1, y1, x2, y2, x3, y3, x4, y4, index, loop = 0;

  // fillColors are used for 'fill' and 'stroke' in the code
  var fillColors = ["#f00", "#ff0", "#00f", "#0ff", "#804"];
  var smallWidth = 10, smallHeight = 40, fbLength, channels;

  var audio   = document.getElementsByTagName("audio")[0];
  var canvas1 = document.getElementsByTagName("canvas")[0];
  var canvas2 = document.getElementsByTagName("canvas")[1];
  var canvas3 = document.getElementsByTagName("canvas")[2];
  var canvas4 = document.getElementsByTagName("canvas")[3];

  var context1 = canvas1.getContext('2d');
  var context2 = canvas2.getContext('2d');
  var context3 = canvas3.getContext('2d');
  var context4 = canvas4.getContext('2d');

  context1.lineWidth = 2; context1.strokeStyle = "#FFFFFF";
  context2.lineWidth = 4; context2.strokeStyle = "#FFFFFF";
  context3.lineWidth = 6; context3.strokeStyle = "#FFFFFF";
  context4.lineWidth = 1; context4.strokeStyle = "#FFFFFF";

  audio.addEventListener("MozAudioAvailable",
writeSamples, false);
  audio.addEventListener("loadedmetadata", getMetadata, false);

  function getMetadata() {
    channels = audio.mozChannels;
    fbLength = audio.mozFrameBufferLength;
  }

  // Render the waveforms
  function writeSamples (event) {
    var data = event.frameBuffer;
    var step = (fbLength / channels) / sampleCount;

    if(loop % 4 == 0) {
       // clear the canvas:
       context1.fillRect(0, 0, rectWidth, rectHeight);
       context1.beginPath();
```

```
            for(var x=1; x<sampleCount; x+= deltaX1){
              barHeight = 2*data[x*step]*rectHeight/2;
              context1.fillStyle = fillColors[x % fillColors.length];
              context1.fillRect(x, rectHeight/2-barHeight,
                                barWidth, barHeight);
            }
        } else if(loop % 4 == 1) {
              context2.strokeStyle = fillColors[loop % fillColors.
length];

              context2.beginPath();
              context2.moveTo(0, rectHeight/2-data[0]*rectHeight/2);

              for(var x=1; x<sampleCount; x++){
         context2.lineTo(x, rectHeight/2-data[x*step]*rectHeight/2);
              }
              context2.stroke();
        } else if(loop % 4 == 2) {
              index = Math.floor(Math.random()*5);

              x1 = (8*loop) % sampleCount;
            y2 = rectHeight/2-data[step*(sampleCount-1)]*rectHeight/2;
            y1 = rectHeight  - (loop % rectHeight);
            x2 = sampleCount - (loop % sampleCount);
            x3 = sampleCount/2;
            y3 = rectHeight/2-data[step*sampleCount/2]*rectHeight/2;

              context3.fillStyle = fillColors[(index+1)%fillColors.
length];
              context3.fillStyle = fillColors[(index+1)%fillColors.
length];
            context3.moveTo(x1, y1);
            context3.quadraticCurveTo(x2, y2, x3, y3);

            context3.fill();
            context3.stroke();
        } else {
    context4.strokeStyle = fillColors[loop % fillColors.length];

            context4.beginPath();
            context4.moveTo(0, rectHeight/2-data[0]*rectHeight/2);

            for(var x=1; x<sampleCount; x+=deltaX4){
              context4.strokeRect(
                        x, rectHeight/2-data[x*step]*rectHeight/2,
                        smallWidth, smallHeight);
            }
            context4.stroke();
        }

        ++loop;
      }
    </script>
  </body>
<html>
```

The graphics effects in Listing 5.8 involve a sine-based bar chart, squiggly lines, a set of Bezier curves, and another set of "fuzzy" random squiggly lines.

Listing 5.8 contains four HTML5 `<canvas>` elements that are used for rendering graphics that are based on the amplitude of the sounds in the audio file. The JavaScript function `writeSamples()` uses the value of the expression `loop%4` to select one of the four HTML5 `<canvas>` element and then render some graphics in that element. Although this rendering is done in a "round robin" fashion, the speed of code execution creates the illusion that the rendering effects is performed simultaneously in all four `<canvas>` elements.

The first part of the code initializes a `channels` variable (which is an object) and the variable `fbLength` (which is the length of the frame buffer of the audio), so that we capture the amplitude of the audio signal that we are sampling, as shown here:

```
function getMetadata() {
    channels = audio.mozChannels;
    fbLength = audio.mozFrameBufferLength;
}
```

The actual graphics images are easy to render, as you can see from the following block of code that computes the height of bar elements based on the values of the audio that are contained in the `data` array (which is pre-populated for us), and then renders a sine-based bar chart:

```
for(var x=1; x<sampleCount; x+= deltaX1){
    barHeight = 2*data[x*step]*rectHeight/2;
    context1.fillStyle = fillColors[x % fillColors.length];
    context1.fillRect(x, rectHeight/2-barHeight,
                      barWidth, barHeight);
}
```

Figure 5.1 displays the result of rendering Listing 5.8 in a Chrome browser on a Macbook.

Note that the code in Listing 5.8 is based on a code sample from this Web site:

http://html5videoguide.net/chapter8.html

Chris Wilson created a Web site that enables you to drag and drop components onto a Web page in order to apply various effects to audio files, and its homepage is here:

https://webaudioplayground.appspot.com/

Chris Wilson is also a co-editor of the W3C Web MIDI API specification:

https://dvcs.w3.org/hg/audio/raw-file/tip/midi/specification.html

Other interesting Web Audio code samples are here:

http://updates.html5rocks.com/2012/02/HTML5-audio-and-the-Web-Audio-API-are-BFFs

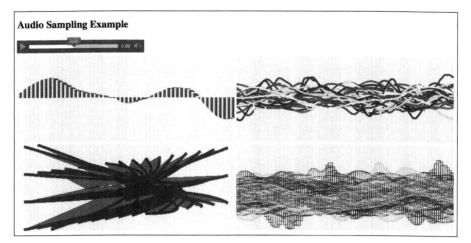

FIGURE 5.1 Converting audio waves into graphics on a Macbook.

http://www.html5audio.org/2012/05/new-google-doodle-uses-web-audio-api.html
http://www.html5rocks.com/en/tutorials/webaudio/positional_audio/
http://chromium.googlecode.com/svn/trunk/samples/audio/index.html
http://jeromeetienne.github.com/slides/webaudioapi/#1
https://bleedinghtml5.appspot.com/#1

SUMMARY

This chapter provided an overview of several HTML5-related techniques for managing and persisting user-provided data using HTML5 Forms. In this chapter, you learned how to perform the following:

- Use the HTML5 `<audio>` and `<video>` elements
- Understand some of the Web Audio APIs

STORAGE, DATABASES, GEOLOCATION, AND OFFLINE APPS

This chapter introduces you to several HTML5 technologies, including about HTML5 Web Storage, Web databases, Geolocation, and offline applications. Web Storage supports LocalStorage for persistent storage and SessionStorage for temporary storage of session-related information. Web databases include WebSQL (which is not covered here because development stopped in November, 2010) and IndexedDB. Geolocation enables users to share their current location, and as you will see later in this chapter, their location may be determined by several methods. Finally, offline Web applications enable users to work on an application even when they are disconnected from the Internet. When users do have access to the Internet, their data changes are synchronized so that everything is in a consistent state.

USING HTML5 WEB STORAGE

The essence of HTML5 Web Storage is that it provides a very simple way to store as key/value pairs, along with a set of APIs for managing your data. In addition to storing simple key/value pairs, you can create a value string consisting of a JSON expression that contains a set of name/value pairs. You can serialize the JSON data before storing it in Web Storage, and then deserialize that JSON data whenever you retrieve it from Web Storage.

Although there is no query language for local storage, you can determine the number of keys in LocalStorage through `localstorage.length`, which you can use as the maximum value for a loop that iterates through the items in LocalStorage. As a simple example, the following code block iterates through the keys in LocalStorage and checks for the values that start with the string Emp:

```
var itemCount = localStorage.length, i=0, key="", value="";

while ( ++i < itemCount ) {
      // retrieve the value of the current key
      key = localStorage.key( i );

      // retrieve the value associated with the current key
      value = localStorage.getItem( key );

      if(value.substr(0,3) == "Emp") {
         // do something with this element
      }
}
```

In addition to storing strings in Web Storage, you can also store JSON data, as shown here:

http://www.codeproject.com/Articles/361428/HTML5-Web-Storage

The advantage of HTML5 Web Storage (both local and session) is the simplicity of the APIs. The disadvantages of HTML5 Web Storage include:

1. An initial platform-specific limit for data
2. No transactional support
3. No query language for accessing structured data

Browsers often have their own mechanism for increasing the amount of available storage after the initial limit is exceeded, but keep in mind that Intel's AppUp has a limited of 150KB for a key/value pair.

HTML5 Web Storage versus IndexedDB

The first advantage of IndexedDB over HTML5 Web Storage is its capacity: IndexedDB has a larger limit (50MB quota in Firefox 4+), and when that limit is exceeded, Firefox prompts the user for permission to increase the maximum size. The manner in which the quota is increased depends on the browser (for desktops and mobile devices), so you need to look into the details for each browser if you are writing a cross-browser application.

The choice between Web Storage and IndexedDB depends on the complexity of your data, the requirements for your application, and whether it's available on your list of target browsers. Later in this chapter, you will see an example of using IndexedDB; its advantages and disadvantages are the opposite of the first two advantages of HTML5 Web Storage that are listed in a previous section.

HTML5 Web Storage versus Cookies

An HTTP cookie is a set of key/value pairs that is used to communicate with a Web server. Cookies are included in an HTTP request header, provided that the cookie data is still valid and the requested domain and path also match the original cookie domain and path. Although cookies are convenient, they do have some drawbacks, such as their size and limits (typically 4K bytes and 300 cookies), performance, and security.

LocalStorage and SessionStorage are intended to provide support for storing a larger amount of data (megabytes instead of kilobytes), storing data beyond a current session, and also support for transactions that occur in multiple browser windows simultaneously, all of which makes HTML5 Web Storage a more powerful technology than cookies.

HTML5 Web Storage and Security

The APIs are subject to the "same origin" policy, in the same way that security is defined for the XMLHTTPRequest object. Origins are determined by domain name (not the underlying IP address), so if you have a unique domain name, you have control over which pages see your data, even on shared hosting. By default, your locally stored data is not shared among subdomains. More information about the "same origin" policy is here:

https://developer.mozilla.org/en/Same_origin_policy_for_JavaScript

The next section contains a code sample that illustrates how to store text strings (consisting of concatenated words) in LocalStorage.

AN EXAMPLE OF HTML5 LOCALSTORAGE

The example in this section uses LocalStorage so that we can persist the data in the multi-lingual dictionary. If you decide to replace local storage with SessionStorage, the data will be available only for the current browser session (hence the name "session storage").

Listing 6.1 displays the contents of `MultiLingualForm2.html` that illustrates how to create and manage our data in LocalStorage.

LISTING 6.1 MultiLingualForm2.html

```
<html lang="en">
<head>
  <meta charset="utf-8" />
  <title>Our Multi-Lingual Dictionary</title>
  <link rel="stylesheet" media="screen" href="MultiLingualForm2.css"
/>

<script>
 function displayItem() {
    var dictionary  = document.forms["dictionary"];
    var english     = dictionary.english.value;
    var storageItem = localStorage.getItem(english);

    var splitItem   = storageItem.split(":");
    var english     = splitItem[0];
    var japanese    = splitItem[1];
    var spanish     = splitItem[2];
    var french      = splitItem[3];
    var italian     = splitItem[4];

    dictionary.english.value  = english;
```

```
        dictionary.japanese.value = japanese;
        dictionary.spanish.value  = spanish;
        dictionary.french.value   = french;
        dictionary.italian.value  = italian;
    }

    function addWord() {
        var dictionary = document.forms["dictionary"];

        var english   = dictionary.english.value;
        var japanese  = dictionary.japanese.value;
        var spanish   = dictionary.spanish.value;
        var french    = dictionary.french.value;
        var italian   = dictionary.italian.value;
        var incomplete = 0;

        var concatenated = english + ":" + japanese + ":" +
                           spanish + ":" + french + ":" +
                           italian;

        if(english == ""||japanese == ""||spanish == ""||
           french == ""||italian == "")
        {
            ++incomplete;
console.log("Skipping incomplete/empty row!");
            return;
        }

        try {
            localStorage.setItem(english, concatenated);
            alert("added new word: "+ concatenated);
            clearFields();

            // append new words to dropdown list
            option = new Option( english );
            wordList.options[wordList.length] = option;
        } catch (e) {
            if (e == QUOTA_EXCEEDED_ERR) {
                alert("Local Storage Quota exceeded");
                // you can clear local storage here:
                //clearLocalStorage();
            }
        }
    }

    function clearFields() {
        var dictionary = document.forms["dictionary"];

        dictionary.english.value  = "";
        dictionary.japanese.value = "";
        dictionary.spanish.value  = "";
        dictionary.french.value   = "";
        dictionary.italian.value  = "";
    }

    function clearLocalStorage() {
```

```
    localStorage.clear();
    populateDropDownList();
  }

  // remove the options from the list
  function removeItemsFromDropDownList() {
    while ( wordList.options.length ) wordList.options[0] = null;
  }

  function createTestData() {
    removeItemsFromDropDownList();
    clearLocalStorage();

    localStorage.setItem("eat", "eat:taberu:comer:manger:mangiare");
    localStorage.setItem("go",  "go:iku:andar:aller:andare");
    localStorage.setItem("buy", "buy:kau:comprar:acheter:comprare");
  }

  function populateDropDownList() {
    // the length property contains the item count in the storage
    var i = -1, key, itemCount, items = {};

    createTestData();
    itemCount = localStorage.length;

// option = new Option( "eat:taberu:comer:manger:mangiare" );
// wordList.options[wordList.length] = option;

    while ( ++i < itemCount ) {
       // retrieve the value of the current key
       key = localStorage.key( i );

       // retrieve the value of the current item
       items[key] = localStorage.getItem( key );

       option = new Option( key );

       // Append to existing options
       wordList.options[wordList.length] = option;
    }

    // Ensure option 0 is selected
    wordList.selectedIndex = 0;
  }
</script>
</head>

<body onLoad="populateDropDownList()">
  <h1>Our Multi-Lingual Dictionary</h1>
  <form id="dictionary" onsubmit="return false;">
  <form>
   <fieldset>
    <div>
      <button id="add" onClick="addWord()">Add New Words</button>
    </div>
    <div>
```

```
      <label for="english">English:</label>
      <input type="text" name="english" id="english" />
   </div>

   <div>
      <label for="japanese">Japanese:</label>
      <input type="text" name="japanese" id="japanese" />
   </div>

   <div>
      <label for="spanish">Spanish:</label>
      <input type="text" name="spanish" id="spanish" />
   </div>

   <div>
      <label for="french">French:</label>
      <input type="text" name="french" id="french" />
   </div>

   <div>
      <label for="italian">Italian:</label>
      <input type="text" name="italian" id="italian" />
   </div>

   <div>
         <button id="clear1" onClick="clearFields()">Clear Input
Fields</button>
      <button id="clear2" onClick="clearLocalStorage()">Clear Local
Storage</button>
   </div>
   <label for="none">The List of Words in Our Dictionary:</label>
   <br />
   <div>
   <select id="wordList" onchange="update()">
     <option value=""></option>
   </select>
   </div>
  </fieldset>
  </form>
</body>
</html>
```

Listing 6.1 contains the JavaScript functions for handling associated functionality. Whenever a new row is added, the JavaScript function addWord() performs a concatenation of the words in that row, with a semi-colon (":") as the delimiter between words, as shown here:

```
var concatenated =  english + ":" + japanese + ":" +
                    spanish + ":" + french + ":" +
                    italian;
```

Next, the concatenated string concatenated is stored as part of a "dictionary" in LocalStorage in a try/catch block with the following line of code:

```
localStorage.setItem(english, concatenated);
```

Keep in mind that the preceding code snippet is equivalent to this snippet:

```
localStorage["eat"] = "eat:taberu:comer:manger:mangiare";
```

Conversely, when the words are retrieved from the dictionary, the JavaScript function `displayItem()` will "split" each concatenated string into the words that are stored in the concatenated string, and then the individual words are displayed in the corresponding language field.

The JavaScript function `displayItem()` displays a word in each input field for each of the specified languages. The JavaScript functions `clearFields()` and `clearLocalStorage()` remove the data from the input fields and from the dictionary in LocalStorage.

Note that each time the HTML page is loaded, the `populateDropDownList()` function is invoked, which creates some test data (via the JavaScript function `createTestData()`) and then populates the dropdown list with the words that are in the dictionary in LocalStorage, as shown here:

```
localStorage.setItem("eat", "eat:taberu:comer:manger:mangiare");
localStorage.setItem("go",  "go:iku:andar:aller:andare");
localStorage.setItem("buy", "buy:kau:comprar:acheter:comprare");
```

Finally, the JavaScript function `removeItemsFromDropDownList()` removes the data from the dropdown list with this line of code:

```
while ( wordList.options.length ) wordList.options[0] = null;
```

LISTING 6.2 MultiLingualForm2.css
```
fieldset {
    float: left;
    border: 2; width: 50%;
    background: #F88;}

div label {
    float: left;
    border: 0; width: 20%;
    background: #FF0;
    -webkit-border-radius: 6px;
    -webkit-box-shadow: 0 0 4px #222222;
}

label {
    float: left;
    border: 0; width: 60%;
    background: #0AD;
    -webkit-border-radius: 6px;
    -webkit-box-shadow: 0 0 4px #222222;
}

input {
    border: 0; width: 40%;
    border: 2px solid white;
    background: #F44;
```

```
        -webkit-border-radius: 6px;
        -webkit-box-shadow: 0 0 4px #333333;
}

button, select {
    font-size: 16px;
    border: 1px solid white;
    background: #CCC;
    -webkit-border-radius: 6px;
    -webkit-box-shadow: 0 0 4px #222222;
    width: 60%;
    padding: 6px;
}
```

Listing 6.2 displays CSS3 selectors for four HTML elements: `fieldset`, `label`, `input`, and the `submit` button. The selectors specify attributes such as the border, width, padding, and rounded corners for the corresponding HTML elements. For example, the CSS3 selector for the HTML `<label>` element specifies yellow (`#FF0`) for the `background` and a `border-radius` of 6 pixels, as shown here:

```
background: #FF0;
-webkit-border-radius: 6px;
```

Similar comments apply to the other CSS selectors in Listing 6. 2, whose content is similar to the CSS selector for the `<label>` element.

Figure 6.1 displays the rendered HTML5 Web page `MultiLingual-Form2.html`, which creates a vivid effect because of the CSS3 selectors in the CSS stylesheet.

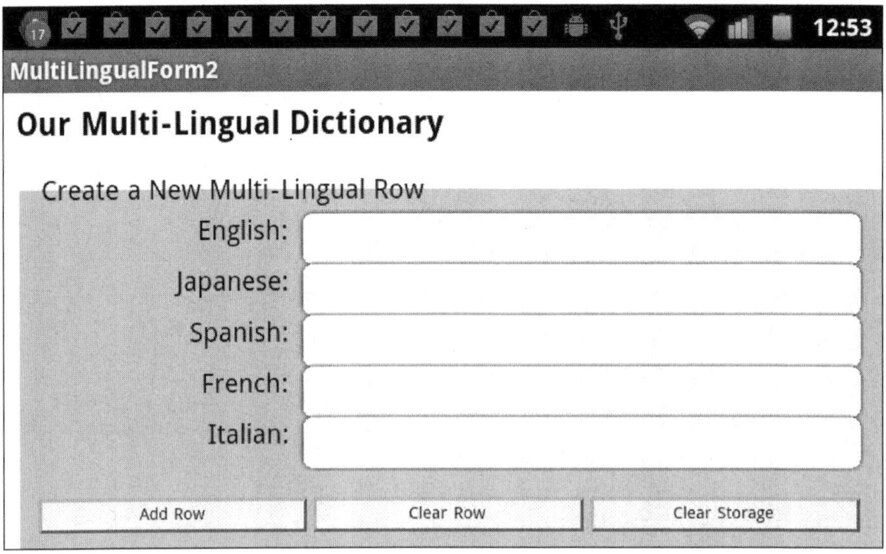

FIGURE 6.1 An HTML5 Form with CSS3 on a Sprint Nexus S 4G with Android ICS

The example in the next section also uses an HTML5 Form that handles data input, but this time the data will be stored in an HTML5 database instead of online LocalStorage.

Incidentally, in addition to storing simple text strings in HTML5 LocalStorage, you can also store images and files, and you can get some useful information and code samples here:

https://hacks.mozilla.org/2012/02/saving-images-and-files-in-localstorage/

You can get the complete code for the preceding article from GitHub:

https://github.com/robnyman/robnyman.github.com/tree/master/ html5demos/localstorage

Note that it's better to store images in IndexedDB because of size limitations for LocalStorage.

HTML5 WEB DATABASES

In addition to using Web Storage for storing data, there are two databases that provide more robust functionality. The database that is actively being developed is IndexedDB, which has not been fully implemented in all modern browsers as this book goes to print.

Another database is WebSQL, but development on this database was discontinued in November, 2010. However, if you have a web application that uses WebSQL, the following article provides useful information to help you migrate to IndexedDB:

http://www.html5rocks.com/en/tutorials/webdatabase/websql-indexeddb/

There are various open source projects available that provide database features for Web applications. For example, html5sql is a JavaScript module that focuses on sequential processing of SQL statements in a transaction. Its homepage is here:

http://html5sql.com/

With html5sql you can process SQL as a single statement string, as an array of strings or objects, or from a separate file that contains SQL statements.

Another open source project is the JavaScript database TaffyDB:

http://taffydb.com/

This open source project includes features such as update and insert, along with cross-browser support, and the ability to extend the database with your own functions. In addition, TaffyDB is compatible with multiple tookits, such as jQuery, YUI, and Dojo.

The next section introduces you to IndexedDB and shows you how to store text strings in an IndexedDB database.

USING AN HTML5 INDEXEDDB DATABASE

In this section, we will use an IndexedDB database to store the data in our multi-lingual dictionary. Listing 6.3 displays selected portions of the contents of the HTML5 Web page `MultiLingualForm2DB1.html` that illustrates how to create and manage our data using an IndexedDB database. Note that Listing 6.3 is available in its entirety on the DVD, as well as the CSS stylesheet `MultiLingualForm2DB1.css` that is referenced in Listing 6.3.

LISTING 6.3 MultiLingualForm2DB1.html

```
<html lang="en">
<head>
  <meta charset="utf-8" />
 <title>Our Multi-Lingual Dictionary with IndexedDB</title>
 // code omitted for brevity

<script>
/* some database-related initialization here */
var dbName = "MultiLingual1";
var multilingual = {};
var indexedDB = window.indexedDB || window.webkitIndexedDB ||
                window.mozIndexedDB || window.moz_indexedDB;

console.log("indexedDB: "+indexedDB);

if ('webkitIndexedDB' in window) {
  window.IDBTransaction = window.webkitIDBTransaction;
  window.IDBKeyRange = window.webkitIDBKeyRange;
  console.log("initializing transaction and range");
}

multilingual.indexedDB = {};
multilingual.indexedDB.db = null;

multilingual.indexedDB.onerror = function(e) {
  console.log(e);
};
```

The preceding code block created an IndexedDB database called `MultiLingual1`, and also checks for the existence of IndexedDB using various browser-specific prefixes, after which the code defines the `onerror()` JavaScript function.

```
multilingual.indexedDB.open = function() {
//console.log("dbName in open: "+dbName);
  var request = indexedDB.open(dbName, 1);

  request.onsuccess = function(e) {
//console.log("top of onsuccess function");
    var v = "1.0";
    multilingual.indexedDB.db = e.target.result;
    var db = multilingual.indexedDB.db;
```

```
      // We can only create Object stores in a setVersion transaction;
      if (v != db.version) {
        var setVrequest = db.setVersion(v);

        // onsuccess is the only place we can create Object Stores
        setVrequest.onerror = multilingual.indexedDB.onerror;

        setVrequest.onsuccess = function(e) {
          if(db.objectStoreNames.contains(dbName)) {
            db.deleteObjectStore(dbName);
          }

          var store = db.createObjectStore(dbName,
                                    {keyPath: "timeStamp"});

          multilingual.indexedDB.getAllWords();
        };
      }
      else {
        multilingual.indexedDB.getAllWords();
      }
    };

  request.onerror = multilingual.indexedDB.onerror;
}
```

The preceding code block defines the open() JavaScript function that opens our database MultiLingual1 that will contain our multilingual information. Version checking is also performed so that we have the flexibility of creating different versions of our database.

```
function addWord() {
  // code omitted for brevity
    var concatenated =  english + ":" + japanese + ":" +
                        spanish + ":" + french + ":" +
                        italian;
  // more code omitted for brevity

  // add new words to our database
  multilingual.indexedDB.addWord(concatenated);
}
```

The preceding block of code contains almost the same code as the corresponding function in Listing 6.3, with the exception of the line of code in bold, which shows you how straightforward it is to add a new row to our IndexedDB multilingual dictionary.

```
multilingual.indexedDB.deleteWord = function(id) {

  var db = multilingual.indexedDB.db;
  var dbNameArray = new Array();
  dbNameArray.push(dbName);

  var trans = db.transaction(dbNameArray, IDBTransaction.READ_WRITE);
  var store = trans.objectStore(dbName);
```

```
var request = store.delete(id);

request.onsuccess = function(e) {
  multilingual.indexedDB.getAllWords();
};

request.onerror = function(e) {
  console.log("Error Adding: ", e);
};
};
```

The preceding block of code shows you how to delete a row in a transaction-oriented manner from an IndexedDB database, where the id represents the row that we want to delete from the database.

Note that only the storage functionality has changed in Listing 6.3, and that when you launch this Web page, it will look identical to Figure 6.1.

WEB DATABASE AND MOBILE DEVICES

You can try to use the same techniques for mobile applications that you use for Web applications, but you will encounter similar constraints in both environments. Although you can use native code to access a database, the solution will be specific to each type of device. The choice that you make depends on the requirements of your application.

One cross-platform solution is to use CouchDB Mobile, which is the mobile version of CouchDB. Another mobile-based alternative is TouchDB, which is a lightweight database engine that is compatible with Apache CouchDB. The creator of TouchDB makes the analogy that "if CouchDB is MySQL, then TouchDB is SQLite." An Android port and an iOS port of TouchDB are available here:

https://github.com/couchbaselabs/TouchDB-Android
https://github.com/couchbaselabs/TouchDB-iOS

GEOLOCATION

Geolocation allows users to share their current location, and their location may be determined by the following methods:

- Cell tower
- GPS hardware on the device
- IP address
- Wireless network connection

The actual method that is used depends on the browser and the capabilities of the device. The browser then determines the location and passes it back to the Geolocation API. Note that the W3C Geolocation specification mentions that there is no guarantee that the Geolocation API returns the device's actual location.

The geolocation object is a child object of window.navigator, and you can check if your browser supports geolocation with the following type of code block:

```
if (window.navigator.geolocation) {
  // geolocation supported
} else {
  // geolocation not supported
}
```

The W3C Geolocation API enables you to obtain geolocation information in a browser session that is running on a device. The Geolocation object is available in the global window.navigator object, accessed via window.navigator.geolocation.

Note that the Geolocation API requires users to allow a Web application to access location information.

The Geolocation object contains the following three methods:

- getCurrentPosition(successCallback, errorCallback, options)
- watchPosition(successCallback, errorCallback, options)
- clearWatch(watchId)

The method getCurrentPosition() tries to get geolocation information, and then calls the first method if it's successful; otherwise, it calls the second method in its argument list.

The method watchPosition() obtains the geolocation at regular intervals; success and failure are handled through the two JavaScript methods in its list of arguments.

Finally, the method clearWatch(watchId) stops the watch process based on the value of watchId.

The major difference between the two methods is that the watchPosition() method will return a value immediately upon being called which uniquely identifies that watch operation.

A table that displays support for Geolocation on desktop and mobile browsers is here:

http://caniuse.com/geolocation

Obtain a User's Position with getCurrentPosition()

The PositionOptions object is an optional parameter that can be passed to the getCurrentPosition() method, which is also an optional parameter to the watchPosition() method. All of the properties in the PositionOptions object are optional as well.

For example, you can define an instance of a PositionOptions object by means of the following JavaScript code block:

```
var options = {
```

```
    enableHighAccuracy: true,
    maximumAge: 60000,
    timeout: 45000
};
```

Next, we can invoke the getCurrentPosition() method by specifying a Java-Script success function, a JavaScript error function, and the previously defined options variable, as shown here:

```
navigator.geolocation.getCurrentPosition(successCallback,
                                         errorCallback,
                                         options);
```

Track a User's Position with watchPosition()

This method is useful when an application requires an updated position each time that a device changes location. The watch operation is an asynchronous operation that is invoked as shown here:

```
var watcher = null;
var options = { enableHighAccuracy: true, timeout: 30000 };

if (window.navigator.geolocation) {
    watcher = navigator.geolocation.watchPosition(
                 successCallback,errorCallback, options);
} else {
    alert('Your browser does not support geolocation.');
}

function successCallback(position) {
    console.log("Success obtaining the device location");
}

// Error obtaining the location
function errorCallback(error) {
    console.log("Error obtaining the device location");
}
```

If your browser supports Geolocation, the JavaScript variable watcher is initialized via an invocation of the watchPosition() method of the geolocation object. Notice that the JavaScript functions success-Callback() and errorCallback() for handling success or failure, respectively (in our case these functions simply display a message in you browser's console).

The W3C Geolocation API provides a method for clearing a watch operation by passing a watchId to the clearWatch() method, as shown here:

```
navigator.geolocation.clearWatch(watcher);
```

After creating a new watch operation you can remove that watch after suc-cessfully retrieving the position of a device, as shown here:

```
var watcher = null;
var options = {enableHighAccuracy: true,timeout: 45000 };
```

```
if (window.navigator.geolocation) {
watcher = navigator.geolocation.watchPosition(successCallback,
        errorCallback, options);
} else {
alert('Your browser does not support geolocation.');
}

function successCallback(position) {
    navigator.geolocation.clearWatch(watcher);
    // Do something with a location here
}
```

As you can see, the JavaScript `successCallback()` function does nothing more than "clearing" the Javascript variable `watcher`; the key point is that you will continue receiving information until you clear this variable.

The DVD contains the HTML Web page `JQGeolocation1.html` that shows you how to use Geolocation with `geoPlugin` (which is not a jQuery plugin):

> *http://www.geoplugin.com*

However, if you prefer to use a jQuery plugin for Geolocation, there are several available, including this one:

> *http://mobile.tutsplus.com/tutorials/mobile-web-apps/html5-geolocation/*

HTML5 OFFLINE WEB APPLICATIONS

The purpose of offline web applications is simple: users can work on an application even when they are disconnected from the Internet. When users do have access to the Internet, their data changes are synchronized so that everything is in a consistent state.

A Web site that contains demos, additional links, and tutorial-like information is here:

> *http://appcachefacts.info/*

The Manifest File

The HTML5 specification requires a so-called "manifest file" (with "appcache" as the suggested suffix) that contains the following three sections:

`CACHE` (the list of files that are going to be cached)
`NETWORK` (the files that can only be accessed online)
`FALLBACK` (specifies the resource to display when users try to access non-cached resources)

As a simple example, Listing 6.4 displays the contents of a sample manifest file called `MyApp.appcache`.

LISTING 6.4 MyApp.appcache

```
CACHE MANIFEST
# Verson 1.0.0
CACHE:
Index.html
Cachedstuff.html
Mystyle.css
Myimage.jpg

NETWORK:
*

FALLBACK:
/ noncached.html
```

You must ensure that the manifest file is served with the following MIME type:

```
text/cache-manifest
```

Second, every Web page that uses offline functionality must reference the manifest file at the top of the Web page:

```
<html lang="en" manifest="mymanifest.manifest">
```

If you have a Web page that is hosted by a provider, you can verify that the Web page contains the correct MIME type by issuing the following type of command:

```
curl -I http://www.myprovider.com/mymanifest.manifest
```

Detecting Online and Offline Status

The simplest way to determine whether or not an application is offline in an HTML5 Web page is with the following code snippet:

```
if(navigator.onLine) {
  // application is online
} else {
  // application is offline
}
For mobile applications that use jQuery Mobile, you can use the
following type of code block:
$(document).bind("offline", function() {
  // application is offline
}
```

Binding the offline event as shown in the preceding code block is useful for handling situations whereby an application goes offline while users are actively viewing an application. In addition, you would send data to a server only when you are online, and store data locally via HTML5 LocalStorage when you are offline.

Another technique for handling online and offline events that works in Firefox 3 (you can test for its support for other browsers) is shown here:

```
document.body.addEventListener("offline", function () {
    // do something here
}, false);

document.body.addEventListener("online", function () {
    // do something else here
}, false);
```

The jQuery plugin jquery-offline is a cross-browser plugin that enables you to use jQuery syntax for offline applications:

https://github.com/wycats/jquery-offline

SUMMARY

This chapter provided an overview of several HTML5-related techniques for managing and persisting user-provided data using HTML5 Forms. In this chapter, you learned how to perform the following:

- Save data in a persistent manner to LocalStorage
- Save data in a persistent manner to an online database
- Understand Geolocation
- Work with offline applications

BROWSER-SERVER COMMUNICATION

This chapter provides an overview of various communication technologies in HTML5, such as AJAX, XHR2, SSE, Web Messaging, and WebSockets. The first part of this chapter discusses CORS (Cross-Origin Resource Sharing), after which the code sample that uses AJAX with XHR2 (XmlHTTPRequest2) will make sense. In addition, the XHR2 section contains three AJAX-related examples, starting with a generic AJAX code sample, followed by a jQuery-based AJAX code sample. The next part of this chapter discusses Web Messaging and SSE, and the final part provides an overview of Web Intents and Web Notifications.

HTML5 CROSS-ORIGIN RESOURCE SHARING (CORS)

In brief, the "same origin policy" allows scripts that originate from the same site to execute, and they can access each other's methods and properties with without restriction. On the other hand, cross-origin resource sharing (CORS) specifies the ways in which a web server can allow its resources to be accessed by web pages from different domains. Although CORS is more flexible than "same origin policy", it does not allow access to resources by any and all requests. In simplified terms, the CORS specification provides support for cross-domain communication by means of a simple header exchange between a client and a server.

Some of the new HTTP headers for the CORS specification are OPTIONS, ORIGIN, and Access-Control-Allow-Origin. When the appropriate CORS headers are provided, CORS makes it possible to make asynchronous HTTP requests to other domains.

The CORS API uses the XMLHttpRequest object as a "container" for sending and receiving the requisite headers for CORS, and also the withCredentials property that can be used for determining programmatically whether or not an XMLHttpRequest object supports CORS.

XMLHTTPREQUEST LEVEL 2 (XHR2)

The `XMLHttpRequest` Level 2 specification supports the following new features:

- Handling byte streams such as `File`, `Blob` and `FormData` objects for upload and download
- Delivering Progress events during upload and download
- Making cross-origin requests
- Making anonymous requests (not HTTPreferer)
- Setting a timeout for the request

Before we look at an XHR2 code sample, we'll start with a code sample that shows you how to make a simple AJAX request, followed by an AJAX request that uses jQuery. Next you will learn about CORS, and the final portion of this section discusses XHR2.

Making AJAX Calls without jQuery

The code sample in this section shows you how to make a "traditional" AJAX call, after which we will look at how to accomplish the same task using jQuery. The purpose of this example is to illustrate the fact that jQuery (once again) enables you to write simpler code that is easier to maintain, debug, and enhance with additional functionality (which you already know from the code samples you have seen throughout this book).

LISTING 7.1 BasicAJAX1.html

```
<!DOCTYPE html>
<html>
<head>
  <meta charset="utf-8" />
  <title>Basic Ajax</title>

  <script>
    var xmlHTTP, myFile = "http://localhost:8080/sample.xml";

    function loadXML(url, callback) {
      if (window.XMLHttpRequest) {
        // Chrome, Firefox, IE7+, Opera, and Safari
        xmlHTTP = new XMLHttpRequest();
      } else {
        // IE5 and IE6
        xmlHTTP = new ActiveXObject("Microsoft.XMLHTTP");
      }

      xmlHTTP.onreadystatechange = callback;
      xmlHTTP.open("GET", url, true);
      xmlHTTP.send();
    }

    function init() {
```

```
      loadXML(myFile, function() {
        if(xmlHTTP.readyState==4 && xmlHTTP.status==200) {
          document.getElementById("myDiv").innerHTML =
                                          xmlHTTP.responseText;
        }
      });
    }
  </script>
</head>

<body onload="init()">
  <div id="myDiv"></div>
</body>
</html>
```

Listing 7.1 contains a JavaScript function `init()` that is executed when the Web page is loaded into a browser. The `init()` function invokes the `loadXML()` function with the name of an XML document, along with a Java-Script function that is executed when the AJAX request is completed.

The `loadXML()` function contains conditional logic that determines how to initialize the JavaScript variable `xmlhttp`, followed by a code block that sets the name of the callback function, specifies a GET method and a URL in the `url` variable (not shown in this code sample), and then makes the actual AJAX request, as shown here:

```
xmlHTTP.onreadystatechange = callback;
xmlHTTP.open("GET", url, true);
xmlHTTP.send();
```

When the AJAX request is completed, the HTML `<div>` element in List-ing 7.1 is updated with the data that is returned by the AJAX request. In this code sample the XML document `sample.xml` is the same file that you saw in Chapter 8, so we will not reproduce its contents here. Refer back to Chapter 8, and you will see that `sample.xml` is an SVG document that contains three SVG-based rectangles, and these rectangles are rendered inside the HTML `<div>` element whose `id` attribute is `myDiv`.

If you are new to AJAX, then this code might seem convoluted (and per-haps confusing). Fortunately, jQuery simplifies the process of making AJAX requests by shielding you from the lower level details, as you will see in the next section.

Making AJAX Calls with jQuery

This example is the modified version of Listing 7.2, which adds jQuery functionality to the code. There are several jQuery methods that provide AJAX-based functionality, including `jQuery.load()`, `jQuery.get()`, and `jQuery.post()`, and `jQuery.ajax()`.

Listing 7.2 displays the contents of `JQueryAJAX1.html` that illustrates how to use the first of these jQuery AJAX methods in an HTML Web page in order to produce the same result as Listing 7.2.

LISTING 7.2: JQueryAjax1.html

```
</script>
<!DOCTYPE html>
<html>
<head>
  <meta charset="utf-8" />
  <title>JQuery Ajax</title>

  <script  src="http://ajax.googleapis.com/ajax/libs/jquery/1.7.1/
jquery.min.js">
  </script>

  <script>
  var url = "http://localhost:8080/sample.xml";

  $(document).ready(function() {
    $("#myDiv").load(url, function() {});
  });
  </script>
</head>

<body>
  <div id="myDiv"></div>
</body>
</html>
```

Listing 7.2 contains a mere one line of code that performs an AJAX request via the jQuery load() method, as shown here:

```
$("#myDiv").load(url, function() {});
```

The result of executing the code in Listing 7.2 is the same as the result of executing the Listing 7.1: the contents of the HTML <div> element whose id attribute is myDiv is replaced with the contents of sample.xml and three SVG-based rectangles are rendered.

Alternatively, you can use the jQuery.ajax() method as shown here:

```
$.ajax({
   url:  url,
   type: "get",
   success: GotData,
   dataType: 'xml'
});
```

In the preceding code block, you also need to define a JavaScript function called GotData() where you would process the result of the AJAX invocation.

As you would expect, jQuery provides much more AJAX functionality. Specifically, jQuery provides support for the following callback hooks:

```
beforeSend()
fail()
dataFilter()
```

```
done()
always()
```

The functions beforeSend(), error(), and done() are intuitively named and they behave as expected. The dataFilter() callback is the first callback to receive data; after it performs its processing, the done() callback is invoked. Finally, the always() callback is invoked, regardless of whether the result of the AJAX invocation was successful or in error.

A concise example of jQuery code that makes an AJAX request using method chaining with several of the preceding APIs is here:

```
// Assign handlers immediately after making the request,
// and get a reference to the jqxhr object for this request
var jqxhr = $.ajax( "example.php" )
    .done(function() { alert("success"); })
    .fail(function() { alert("error"); })
    .always(function() { alert("complete"); });

// perform other work here ...

// Set another completion function for the request above
jqxhr.always(function() { alert("second complete"); });
```

If you want to explore more AJAX-related features in jQuery, a complete list of jQuery AJAX methods is here:

http://api.jquery.com/category/ajax/
http://api.jquery.com/ajaxComplete/

This chapter contains one more AJAX-based code sample that users XHR2, but first we need to discuss CORS and some of the features that it provides in HTML5.

AJAX Requests Using XMLHttpRequest Level 2 (XHR2)

Listing 7.3 displays AjaxForm.html, which illustrates how to create an HTML5 Web page that uses the new FormData object XHR2.

LISTING 7.3 AjaxForm.html

```
<!doctype html>
<html lang="en">

<head>
  <meta charset="utf-8" />
 <title>Ajax Form</title>

 <script>
  function sendForm(form) {
    var formData = new FormData(form);

    var xhr = new XMLHttpRequest();
    xhr.open('POST', form.action, true);
    xhr.onload = function(e) {
```

```
      // do something here
    };

    xhr.send(formData);

    // Prevent page submission
    return false;
  }
 </script>
</head>

<body>
<form id="myform" name="myform" action="xhr2.php">
  <input type="text"   name="uname" value="asmith">
  <input type="number" name="id"    value="33333">
  <input type="submit" onclick="return sendForm(this.form);">
</form>
</body>
</html>
```

Listing 7.3 is straightforward. The `<body>` element contains a HTML `<form>` element with several input fields. Next, the form data is submitted via the JavaScript function `sendForm()` that creates a `FormData` object and then submits the user-provided data via XHR2, as shown in this code block:

```
var xhr = new XMLHttpRequest();
xhr.open('POST', form.action, true);
xhr.onload = function(e) {
    // do something here
};
xhr.send(formData);
```

The `XMLHttpRequest` Level 2 specification supports the transfer of binary data and tracks the upload progress through the `XMLHttpRequestUpload` object; consequently, XHR2 can be used for binary file transfers via the File APIs and the `FormData` object.

If you need to use XHR2 in your HTML Web pages, there is an XHR2 library here:

https://github.com/p-m-p/xhr2-lib

More tutorials and information regarding XHR2 are here:

http://www.html5rocks.com/en/tutorials/file/xhr2/
http://www.matiasmancini.com.ar/jquery-plugin-ajax-form-validation-html5.html

HTML5 WEBSOCKETS

The purpose of WebSockets is to provide a bi-directional channel over a single TCP socket. WebSockets is designed for Web browsers and Web servers, but it can actually be used by other client or server applications.

A clarification is in order regarding two technologies for channel-based communication. SSE (Server-Sent Events) is another HTML5 technology that is used for communication (and also covered later in this chapter), but there's a major difference between SSE and WebSockets. Both of these are capable of pushing data to browsers, but SSE connections can only push data to the browser, whereas WebSockets connections can both send data to the browser and receive data from the browser. Applications that send online stock quotes or update a Twitter timeline can benefit from SSE; on the other hand, a chat application can benefit from WebSockets.

Although SSE and WebSockets are not competing technologies, the functionality of SSE is a subset of the functionality that is available in WebSockets; however, keep in mind that browser support for WebSockets appears to be greater than the corresponding support for SSE.

You can programmatically test for WebSocket support in any browser by including the following code block in an HTML5 Web page:

```
if(window.WebSocket) {
  alert("WebSockets is supported.");
} else {
  alert("WebSockets is supported.");
}
```

These links will report WebSockets support in your browser:

http://jsconsole.com/?WebSocket
http://websockets.org/

In addition, you can check the *www.caniuse.com* Web site for browser support for WebSockets.

Listing 7.4 displays the contents of `WebSockets2.html` that illustrates how to make a Web request from an HTML5 Web page to a WebSocket server.

LISTING 7.4 WebSockets2.html

```
<!DOCTYPE HTML>
<html lang="en">
<head>
  <meta charset="utf-8" />
 <title>HTML5 Web Sockets </title>

<script>
function WebSocketTest() {
   if ("WebSocket" in window) {
      alert("WebSocket is supported by your Browser");

      // Open a web socket...
      var ws = new WebSocket("ws://localhost:9998/echo");

      ws.onopen = function() {
         // send data using send()
         ws.send("Message to send");
         alert("Message is sent...");
```

```
    };

    ws.onmessage = function (evt) {
        var received_msg = evt.data;
        alert("Received message: "+received_msg);
    };

    ws.onclose = function() {
        // websocket is closed
        alert("Connection is closed...");
    };

    ws.onerror = function(evt) {
        console.log("Error occurred: "+evt.data);
    };
    } else {
        // The browser doesn't support WebSocket
        alert("WebSocket not supported by your Browser");
    }
}
</script>
</head>

<body>
<div id="sse">
    <a href="javascript:WebSocketTest()">Run WebSocket</a>
</div>
</body>
</html>
```

Listing 7.4 contains the JavaScript function `WebSocketTest()` that defines all of the WebSocket code, starting with conditional logic that checks for WebSocket support in your browser. If WebSockets are supported, then one line of code initializes the JavaScript variable `ws`, which references a WebSocket at a specific port number, as shown here:

```
var ws = new WebSocket("ws://localhost:9998/echo");
```

The remaining code defines handlers for `open` (which makes a request to the server), `message` (which handles messages received from the server), `close` (which closes the connection), and `error` (which reports error messages).

The next section shows you a simple example of using WebSockets to update the contents of an HMTL5 Web page.

A Simple WebSocket Web Page

Listing 7.5 displays the contents of `WSTestSupport2.html` that illustrates how to make a WebSocket invocation at `ws://echo.websocket.org`, which is a well-known endpoint that specifies the `ws` protocol instead of the `http` protocol.

LISTING 7.5 WSTestSupport2.html

```html
<!doctype html>
<html lang="en">
<head>
  <meta charset="utf-8" />
  <title>Client-Side WebSocket Invocation</title>

  <script>
    // http://websocket.org/echo.html
    var wsUri = "ws://echo.websocket.org/";
    var websocket;

    function init() {
      testWebSocket();
    }

    function testWebSocket() {
      websocket = new WebSocket(wsUri);

      websocket.onopen    = onOpen;
      websocket.onclose   = onClose;
      websocket.onmessage = onMessage;
      websocket.onerror   = onError;
    }

    function onOpen(evt) {
      var msg = "Hello from Web Sockets Client";

      console.log("CONNECTED");
      websocket.send(msg);
      console.log("SENT: "+mmsg);
    }

    function onClose(evt) {
      console.log("DISCONNECTED");
    }

    function onMessage(evt) {
      console.log("RESPONSE: "+evt.data);
      websocket.close();
    }

    function onError(evt) {
      console.log("ERROR: "+evt.message);
    }

    window.onload("init()");

  </script>
</head>

<body>
  <h2>WebSocket Test</h2>
</body>
</html>
```

Listing 7.5 contains HTML markup and the JavaScript function `init()` that is executed after the Web page is loaded into a browser. The `init()` function first finds the HTML `<div>` element whose `id` attribute has value `output`, and then it defines a set of event handlers for multiple socket-related callbacks, as shown here:

```
function testWebSocket() {
    websocket = new WebSocket(wsUri);
    websocket.onopen = function(evt) { onOpen(evt) };
    websocket.onclose = function(evt) { onClose(evt) };
    websocket.onmessage = function(evt) { onMessage(evt) };
    websocket.onerror = function(evt) { onError(evt) };
}
```

As you can see, the JavaScript functions in the preceding code block are defined in Listing 7.5, and each function reports its results by appending an HTML `<p>` element to the Web page with the following JavaScript function:

```
function writeToScreen(message) {
    var pre = document.createElement("p");
    pre.style.wordWrap = "break-word";
    pre.innerHTML = message;
    output.appendChild(pre);
}
```

You can find additional information about WebSockets in the W3C specification:

http://dev.w3.org/html5/websockets/

You can download a free copy (PDF) of the DZone Reference Card for WebSockets here:

http://refcardz.dzone.com/refcardz/html5-websocket

MIGRATING TO HTML5 WEBSOCKETS

Every application maintains state in some form, and in server-side Web applications, the server has to do extra work to maintain state because HTTP is stateless, intended as a fire-and-forget way to retrieve documents, and browsers were optimized as rendering platforms, not as uniform application platforms.

Richard Clark[1] points out that although state can be stored in the client or on the server, keep in mind the existence of XSS exploits, which suggests that server-side state might be a weaker solution. The question of which side maintains state (client or server) is more a question of trust: if the data has to be managed securely, it's held on the server side (inside the trust boundary.) However, something like a shopping cart can be safely held on either side; in fact, you *want* to keep as much of the state on the client as possible to improve responsiveness and post updates to the server asynchronously. See the following link for more details:

---

[1] Richard Clark is the technical reviewer of this book.

http://alexmaccaw.com/posts/async_ui

An interesting white paper on the topic ("Building Living Web Applications") is here:

http://kaazingcorp.cachefly.net/com/file/Kaazing-WP-Living-Web-Architecture-Mar-2012.pdf

Richard Clark also suggests that people will not migrate simply for the sake of migration; rather, they will build a next-generation application using WebSocket when there is sufficient need for an alternative to HTTP-based methods in order to provide more robust functionality.

Given the benefits of WebSockets, you might be wondering if there are ways to speed up current systems to emulate some of the benefits of WebSockets. For example, suppose someone sets up a Unix/Linux machine to handle 50K connections, installs Apache, and sets the "keep-alive" header. This configuration is akin to a "poor man's SPDY server," and it's important to keep in mind that the difference between WebSockets and HTTP is more than the use of "keep-alive."

A comparison between highly optimized Comet and stock WebSocket (note the 50K case on both sides) is here:

http://webtide.intalio.com/2011/09/cometd-2-4-0-websocket-benchmarks/

Incidentally, cookies are still valid for storing tiny bits of data that need to be sent back to the server with every request. Specifically, they can also be sent when establishing a WebSocket connection, which also helps maintain interoperability with systems that expect cookies on a request (such as legacy single sign-on systems).

AVAILABLE WEBSOCKET SERVERS

There are many WebSocket servers available, written in languages such as Java, JavaScript, Ruby, Python, and C++. Some of the popular ones include NodeJS, Kaazing, and mod_pyWebSocket, and you can perform an Internet search to find many others.

The following link lists the support for WebSockets in modern browsers (desktop and also mobile):

http://caniuse.com/#search=websocket

A list of WebSocket servers is here:

http://www.slideshare.net/fullscreen/peterlubbers/html5-realtime-and-connectivity/55

A tabularized display that itemizes the feature support for multiple WebSocket servers is here (but be sure to read the caveats at the top of this Web page):

http://en.wikipedia.org/wiki/Comparison_of_WebSocket_implementations

Another important point to keep in mind is that the WS standard went through multiple iterations; developers often implemented one of the interim versions before settling on the final protocol. Thus, the WS implementation that you select may need to support an older protocol as well as the latest until the majority of devices catch up.

USING HTML5 SERVER-SENT EVENTS (SSE)

SSE is an HTML5 technology for sending data from a server to a client after the initial client connection has been established. This one-way communication from a server to a client is useful in cases where you need to send message updates or data streams.

Keep in mind that SSE is a "push" from the server to the client, which is the opposite of a client "pull" from a server. Second, you might be thinking that SSE is "half" of WebSockets in the sense that there is no communication from the client to the server.

The SSE specification requires message IDs and reconnection on the server side, whereas the client-side API is essentially identical to WebSocket.

SSE uses the JavaScript EventSource API, which clients use in order to request a URL and then receive a series of events, as shown in Listing 7.6.

LISTING 7.6 EventSource1.html

```
<html>
   <head>
    <meta charset="utf-8" />
     <title>SSE Event Source </title>

     <script>
         var source = new EventSource('Events');
         source.onmessage = function (event) {
            ev = document.getElementById('events');
            ev.innerHTML += "<br>[in] " + event.data;
         };
     </script>
   </head>
   <body>
     <div id="events"></div>
   </body>
</html>
```

Listing 7.6 contains HTML markup and some JavaScript code that starts by instantiating a JavaScript variable `source` that is a reference to an `Event-Source` object, followed by a block of code for the callback function that processes the data that is received from the server, as shown here:

```
source.onmessage = function (event) {
   ev = document.getElementById('events');
   ev.innerHTML += "<br>[in] " + event.data;
};
```

The preceding code block simply appends the latest information from the server, which is available in `event.data`, to the HTML `<div>` element whose `id` attribute has the value `events`.

Prior to HTML5 SSE "server push" technologies were employed to provide the functionality that is available in HTML5 SSE. In particular, Comet is a popular model that can be implemented by "long polling," whereby a server maintains an HTTP request from a client in order to periodically send data to the client.

However, the original Comet document did not specify an implementation, which means that in practice you don't know whether a given Comet implementation uses polling, long polling, or HTTP streaming (or perhaps something else). Each of these approaches places different demands on the infrastructure, whereas SSE is standardized on HTTP streaming, which provides consistency.

Incidentally, other terms for Comet include "AJAX push," "Reverse AJAX," and "HTTP server push." More information about Comet is here:

http://en.wikipedia.org/wiki/Push_technology

*http://en.wikipedia.org/wiki/Comet_(programming)*Listing 7.7 displays the contents of the HTML5 Web page `HTML5SSE1.html` that illustrates how to use HTML5 SSE.

LISTING 7.7: HTML5SSE1.html

```
<!DOCTYPE html>
<html>
<head>
  <meta charset="utf-8" />
  <title>Server Sent Events (SSE)</title>

  <script>
  function SetupSSE() {
   //check for browser support
   if(typeof(EventSource) !== "undefined") {
console.log("Browser supports EventSource");

     // create an EventSource object with the name
     // and the location of the server-side script
     var eSource = new EventSource("echo");
//console.log("eSource: "+eSource);

     // receive server-side messages
     eSource.onmessage = function(event) {
console.log("Processing data from server...");
      // display the data from the server
      document.getElementById("serverData").innerHTML = event.data;
     };
   }
   else {
console.log("Browser does not support EventSource");
      document.getElementById("serverData").innerHTML =
                       "No support for server-sent events.";
   }
```

```
  }
  </script>
</head>

<body onload="SetupSSE();">
  <div id="serverData"> </div>
</body>
</html>
```

Listing 7.7 invokes the JavaScript function `SetupSSE()` after the Web page is loaded into a browser. After confirming that the `EventSource` object is non-null, this function instantiates the JavaScript variable `eSource` to communicate with the server-side program called "echo," as shown here:

```
var eSource = new EventSource("echo");
```

Next, the `SetupSSE()` function defines a function for the `onmessage` event that updates an HTML `<div>` element in the client with data that is received from the server, as shown here:

```
eSource.onmessage = function(event) {
  // display the data from the server
  document.getElementById("serverData").innerHTML = event.data;
};
```

As an example, in Python 2.x you can start a Python-based HTTP server typing the following command (you can replace [portnumber] with a port number other than the default port 8000):

```
python -m SimpleHTTPServer [portnumber]
```

In Python 3, you can use the following command:

```
python -m http.server [portnumber]
```

After a few moments you will see the following message:

```
Serving HTTP on 0.0.0.0 port 8000 ...
```

In Listing 7.7, you also need a program on the server called `echo` that periodically sends data to the browser that has established a connection with the server.

Additional information about HTML5 server-sent events is available in the W3C specification:

http://dev.w3.org/html5/eventsource/

A Comparison of AJAX and SSE

In the previous section, we briefly contrasted SSE with WebSockets, and you might also be wondering about AJAX versus SSE. Some of the advantages of SSE are here:

- One long-lived HTTP connection is required
- Well-supported in modern browsers
- Simpler and "cleaner" client-side implementation
- Designed "from the ground up" to be efficient

Since one persistent connection is required for each client, a large number of clients will result in many open connections on the server, and your server needs to be able to handle such a volume. On the other hand, AJAX polling adds a lot of HTTP overhead due to the process of establishing and then "tearing down" HTTP connections.

Keep in mind that a "bullet list" of features will only provide you with guidelines for helping you select the most suitable technology for the task that you are trying to solve. It's a good idea to get feedback regarding proposed solutions from someone who has the requisite experience.

Incidentally, if you use an IE browser, you can perform an Internet search to find a jQuery plugin that will provide SSE support in your browser. In addition, since SSE uses an established technique (HTTP streaming), implementers could create a compatible library using older APIs.

WHAT IS SPDY?

SPDY (pronounced "speedy") is an experimental protocol developed by Google, and it's intended to enhance HTTP to make synchronous HTTP requests faster, as described in the SPDY whitepaper:

http://www.chromium.org/spdy/spdy-whitepaper

Although SPDY is not an official part of HTML, it's included in this chapter because it could become useful for your Web applications (and if this turns out not to be the case, it's still useful information for you).

SPDY adds a layer between HTTP and SSL that allows for multiple concurrent streams over a single TCP connection. SPDY Push is a technique that sends multiple files (such as JavaScript, CSS, and images in a Web page) in a single request, which can reduce the round trip time. Thus, SPDY does not replace HTTP; its purpose is to modify the way HTTP requests and responses are sent "over the wire."

NOTE By contrast, WebSockets is an alternative to HTTP that supports bidirectional real time communication; in fact, WebSockets and SPDY are complementary protocols. WebSockets makes its initial handshake with servers over HTTP to determine whether or not the ws:// protocol is supported, whereas SPDY's primary methods of optimization is compressing and caching HTTP request headers.

At this point, the performance gains through SPDY depend on various factors (discussed in the link by Guy Podjarny below). On one hand, the SPDY whitepaper asserts that performance gains can be significant:

"Header compression resulted in an ~88% reduction in the size of request headers and an ~85% reduction in the size of response headers...We found a reduction of 45–1142 ms in page load time simply due to header compression."

On the other hand, Guy Podjarny of Akamai performed a set of tests on "real world" websites and concluded that SPDY did not offer significant performance improvements, as documented here:

http://www.guypo.com/technical/not-as-spdy-as-you-thought/

Both Chrome and Firefox support SPDY, and Twitter now supports SPDY on its servers.

HTML5 WEB INTENTS

Web Intents is an upcoming framework that provides Web-based communication between applications as well as service discovery. Web Intents provides a discovery mechanism and a lightweight RPC mechanism, modeled after the Intents system in Android.

One of the advantages of Web Intents is that it enables Web applications to communicate with each other, without requiring them to know each other's identity. Google Chrome 18+ natively supports Web Intents, and there is a JavaScript shim with support for IE 8+ (and other browsers).

The proposed method of intent registration is via the intent tag, as shown here:

```
<intent
  action="http://webintents.org/share"
  type="image/*"
  href="share.html"
  disposition="window|inline"
/>
```

An invocation of an `Intent` is shown here:

```
var intent = new Intent("http://webintents.org/share",
                        "text/uri-list",
                        "http://news.bbc.co.uk");

window.navigator.startActivity(intent);
```

Additional information about Web Intents is here:

http://webintents.org/

http://dvcs.w3.org/hg/web-intents/raw-file/tip/spec/Overview.html
A video demo of Web Intents by Robin Berjon is here:
*https://docs.google.com/file/d/0B-2pb_m94nPxRGV5LTRvM0pLaUU/
edit?pli=1*

HTML5 WEB MESSAGING

Web Messaging enables documents to share information without exposing their underlying DOM structure, which reduces the risk from malicious cross-origin scripts. Web Messaging actually involves *cross-document messaging* and *channel messaging*. Cross-document messaging uses the window. postMessage() function, and channel messaging is also known as MessageChannel.

Keep in mind that the Web Messaging API is different from the Messaging API (WD status) that defines a high-level interface to messaging functionality, including SMS, MMS, and e-mail.

Web Messaging, SSE, and WebSockets are the three primary communication interfaces that are available in HTML5, and all three technologies involve message events. The structure of a message is specified by the MessageEvent interface (which inherits from the DOM Event interface) that contains five read-only attributes: data (a string sent from the originating script), origin (such as *http://www.acme.com:12345*), lastEventId (a string that uniquely identifies the current message event), ports (an array of MessagePort objects that are sent with a message), and source (which references the window of the originating document).

There are two points to keep in mind. The first is that Web Messaging, SSE, and WebSockets do not use all the fields in a message event, and if you are interested in the detail regarding these differences, you can get that information from section 10 of the specification:

http://www.whatwg.org/specs/web-apps/current-work/#comms

The second point is that message events do not have a default action, do not "bubble," and are not cancelable. As a simple example, suppose that you want to send a message from the parent document to a document contained in an IFRAME that is hosted on another server. Web Messaging makes this type of communication possible by passing data as a message event, where the "send" code from the parent to the IFRAME would look something like the following:

```
var iframe = document.querySelector('iframe');
var button = document.querySelector('button');
var clickHandler = function() {
// iframe.contentWindow refers to the iframe's window object iframe.
contentWindow.postMessage('The message to send.',
                          'http://dev.opera.com');}
button.addEventListener('click',clickHandler,false);
```

The "receive" code that handles the message sent from the IFRAME back to the parent would look like this:

```
var messageEventHandler = function(event) {
    // check that the origin is correct:
```

```
    if(event.origin == 'http://dev.opera.com'){
       alert(event.data);
    }
}

window.addEventListener('message', messageEventHandler,false);
```

For more information, navigate to the W3C Web Messaging specification here:

http://www.w3.org/TR/webmessaging/

HTML5 WEB NOTIFICATIONS

The Notifications API allows you to display notifications to users for given events. You can display notifications in various ways, including e-mail messages, tweets, or calendar events.

You can easily check for notifications support in your browser with this code block, whose conditional logic checks for the presence of `window.notifications` and `window.webKitNotifications` (which you can expand to include prefixes):

```
if(window.webkitNotifications ||
   window.notifications) {
   console.log("Notifications are supported.");
}
else {
   console.log("Notifications are not supported.");
}
```

Notification objects dispatch events during their lifecycle, which you can use to generate desired behavior. For example, the `show` event occurs whenever a notification is shown to users, and the following code snippet illustrates how to display a notification for 15 seconds:

```
new Notification("New Email Received",
           { iconUrl: "mail.png",
             onshow: function(){
                    setTimeout(notification.close(), 15000);
                    }
           });
```

The `close` event occurs when users dismiss a notification, and the following code snippet shows you how to ensure that additional reminders are suppressed:

```
new Notification("Meeting about to begin",
              { iconUrl: "calendar.gif",
                body: "Room 101",
                onclose: function() { cancelReminders(event); }
              });
```

For more information, navigate to the W3C Web Notifications draft specification here:

http://www.w3.org/TR/notifications/

You can find working code samples that illustrate how to grant permissions to a Web site to display notifications here:

http://www.html5rocks.com/en/tutorials/notifications/quick/

The preceding Web site contains a code sample that shows you the ease with which new Twitter tweets can be displayed in a Web page.

SUMMARY

This chapter provided an overview of various HTML5 technologies and grouped them according to their current W3C status. For your convenience, these HTML5 technologies are listed alphabetically below:

- AJAX (XHR2)
- WebSockets
- Server-sent events (SSE)
- SPDY
- Web Intents, Messaging, and Notifications

In this chapter, you saw how to test browsers for WebSocket support, and how to make a WebSocket invocation. In addition, you saw how to use jQuery in conjunction with various HTML5-related technologies.

MISCELLANEOUS HTML5 APIS

The first part of this chapter introduces you to Microformats, which differ from other HTML5 technologies in the sense that they do not provide a set of APIs. The second part of this chapter discusses HTML5 Drag and Drop (DnD). You will see a jQuery-based code sample that illustrates drag and drop for JPG files (which is simpler than "pure" HTML5 Drag and Drop APIs), an example of invoking some of the HTML5 File APIs in jQuery. The third part of this chapter delves into some technologies for WebGL, including Three.js and tQuery (a jQuery plugin for Three.js). The fourth part of this chapter discusses File APIs and the History API, and the final portion briefly discusses some useful tools for performance. If you are unfamiliar with jQuery, you can read one of the appendices, which will enable you to understand the code samples in this book that use jQuery.

USING HTML5 MICRODATA

Unlike the other HTML5 technologies in this chapter, HTML5 Microdata does not provide JavaScript APIs. Microdata provides a standardized way to include additional semantics in HTML5 Web pages. Even if this technology is not important to you now, it's worth skimming through the material in this section so that you are aware of its purpose in case you need to use this technology at some point in the future. Keep in mind that HTML5 Microdata is markup only, and unlike other HTML5 technologies, there are no APIs available.

There are many specialized types of microformats that provide information about different types of entities. Some of the more common microformats include Breadcrumbs (displays the location of a given page relative to the structure of a Web site), Businesses and Organizations (for corporate structure and related contact information), Events (provides calendar data), Product Information (provides product catalog data), People (provides information about people, such as contact information).

Microdata defines five HTML attributes that can be applied to any HTML5 tag, where each attribute is essentially a name/value pair. The most commonly used tags are `itemscope`, `itemtype`, and `itemprop`, whereas `itemref` and `itemid` are not needed by most common formats.

Microdata also supports customized elements and allows you to embed custom properties in HTML5 Web pages. Each group is called an *item*, and each name-value pair is a *property*. Items and properties are represented by regular elements. You can create an item using the `itemscope` attribute and add a property to an item using the `itemprop` attribute on one of the item's descendants.

As a simple example, the following code block contains two items, each of which has the property "name:"

```
<div itemscope>
<p>My name is <span itemprop="name">Zara</span>.</p>
</div>

<div itemscope>
<p>My name is <span itemprop="name">Nuha</span>.</p>
</div>
```

For additional information, navigate to the W3C Microdata specification (currently a work in progress):

http://dev.w3.org/html5/md/

You can also find Google's currently supported Microdata formats here:

http://www.google.com/support/webmasters/bin/topic.py?topic=21997

If you want to write HTML5 Web pages with Microdata functionality using jQuery, you can find a jQuery plugin for Microdata here:

http://www.vanseodesign.com/web-design/html5-microdata/

HTML5 DRAG AND DROP (DND)

HTML5 Drag and Drop enables you to rearrange the layout of HTML elements in an HTML Web page. HTML4 does not have built-in support for DnD, and creating such support requires considerably more JavaScript code than a toolkit such as jQuery.

On the other hand, HTML5 provides Drag and Drop APIs that support Drag and Drop in HTML5 Web pages. HTML5 Drag and Drop supports the following events:

```
drag
dragend
dragenter
dragleave
```

```
dragover
dragstart
drop
```

In addition, the HTML5 DnD provides a source element, the data content, and the target, which represent the drag "start" element, the data that is being dragged, and the "target" element, respectively.

In your HTML5 Web page, you attach event listeners to elements, as shown here:

```
myElement.addEventListener('dragenter', handleDragEnter, false);
myElement.addEventListener('dragleave', handleDragLeave, false);
myElement.addEventListener('dragover',  handleDragOver,  false);
myElement.addEventListener('dragstart', handleDragStart, false);
```

Next, you define custom code in each of the JavaScript event handlers that will be executed whenever the associated event occurs.

However, keep in mind that HTML5 Web pages with DnD functionality still require browser-specific code, which means that you need to maintain the code in multiple HTML5 Web pages if you want to support multiple browsers.

Eric Bidelman has written an extensive and detailed blog entry that shows you how to write an HTML5 Web page with Drag and Drop functionality:

http://www.html5rocks.com/en/tutorials/dnd/basics/

We will skip examples of "native" HTML5 DnD and proceed to an example of using jQuery with HTML5 DnD, which is covered in the next section.

JQUERY AND HTML5 DRAG AND DROP

Drag and Drop is exceptionally simple in jQuery: only one line of code is required for an HTML element.

Listing 8.1 displays the contents of the HTML5 Web page JQDragAnd-Drop1.html, which illustrates how easy it is to create an HTML5 Web page with Drag and Drop using jQuery.

LISTING 8.1 JQDragAndDrop1.html

```
<!doctype html>
<html lang="en">
<head>
  <meta charset="utf-8" />
 <title>JQuery DnD</title>

<style>
 div[id^="draggable"] {
   position:relative; width: 100px; height: 100px;
 }

 #draggable1 { background: red; }
 #draggable2 { background: yellow; }
 #draggable3 { background: blue; }
```

```
</style>

<script src="http://ajax.googleapis.com/ajax/libs/jquery/1.7.1/jquery.
min.js">
</script>

<script
src="http://ajax.googleapis.com/ajax/libs/jqueryui/1.8.9/jquery-
ui.min.js">
</script>

<script
  $(document).ready(function() {
    $('#draggable1').draggable();
    $('#draggable2').draggable();
    $('#draggable3').draggable();
  });
</script>
</head>

<body>
  <div id="content" style="height: 400px;">
    <div id="draggable1">
        <img src="Laurie1.jpeg" width="100" height="100" />
    </div>
    <div id="draggable2">
        <img src="Laurie2.jpeg" width="100" height="100" />
    </div>
    <div id="draggable3">
        <img src="Laurie3.jpeg" width="100" height="100" />
    </div>
  </div>
</body>
</html>
```

Listing 8.1 contains a block of jQuery code that makes three HTML `<div>` elements (which are defined in the `<body>` element) draggable using this type of code snippet:

```
$('#draggable2').draggable();
```

The `<body>` element contains three `<div>` elements, each of which contains a JPEG image that you can drag around the screen.

Figure 8.1 displays the result of rendering Listing 8.1 in a Chrome browser on a Macbook.

Figure 8.2 shows an example of dragging the images in Listing 8.1 to different positions in a Chrome browser on a Macbook.

More information about jQuery Drag and Drop (including the list of available options) is available here:

http://jqueryui.com/demos/draggable/

There are several jQuery plugins for drag and drop functionality that are listed here:

*http://plugins.jquery.com/projects/
plugins?type=45*

You can also use jQuery Mobile with HTML5 DnD, and although we will not discuss an example, you can perform an Internet search to find tutorials and code examples, or you can start with the details in this link:

*http://www.jsplugins.com/Scripts/Plugins/View/
Jquery-Mobile-Drag-And-Drop/*

JQUERY AND HTML5 FILE APIS

The HTML5 File APIs enable you to create, read, and write files on the file system. The first step is to obtain access to the HTML5 FileSystem, after which you can perform file-related operations. You can read about these APIs and also see code examples here:

*http://aquantum-demo.appspot.com/file-upload
http://www.htmlgoodies.com/html5/other/
responding-to-html5-filereader-events.html*

The DVD contains the HTML Web page `JQ-FileInfo1.html` that illustrates how to use jQuery in order to display the attributes of a file that is selected by users. A more interesting (and more useful) example is `JQFileUpload2.html` in Listing 8.2 that illustrates how to use jQuery and XHR2 to upload files.

FIGURE 8.1 Three images in a Chrome browser on a Macbook

FIGURE 8.2 Three dragged images in a Chrome browser on a Macbook

LISTING 8.2: JQFileUpload2.html

```
<!DOCTYPE HTML>
<html lang="en">
 <head>
   <meta charset="utf-8" />
   <title>File Upload with XHR2</title>
    <script src="http://ajax.googleapis.com/ajax/libs/jquery/1.7.1/
jquery.min.js">
   </script>
 </head>

 <body>
  <script>
   $(document).ready(function () {
      $("body").on("change", '#fileUploader', function() {
         // Prepare post data
         var data = new FormData();
         data.append('uploadfile', this.files[0]);

         // invoke the jQuery .ajax method:
         $.ajax({
           type: 'POST',
           url: url,
           data: data,
           success:  function(data) {
                       // do something here
                     },
           dataType: 'text'
         });
      });
    });
  </script>

  <div>
    <input id="fileUploader" type="file" multiple />
  </div>
 </body>
</html>
```

Listing 8.2 contains an HTML `<input>` field that enables uses to select a file from the file system. After a file is selected, the jQuery "change" event is triggered, and an XHR2 `FormData` object (discussed earlier in this chapter) is created and populated, as shown here:

```
var data = new FormData();
data.append('uploadfile', this.files[0]);
```

The selected file is uploaded via the jQuery `.ajax()` method, which contains a "success" function that is invoked after the AJAX request has been completed successfully.

If you want to use a jQuery plugin for uploading files in HTML5 Web pages, there are several available, such as the cross-browser jQuery plugin jquery-filedrop. Its homepage is here:

https://github.com/weixiyen/jquery-filedrop

HTML5 HISTORY APIS

One key reason for the new History APIs is the ability to update the URL (the location) without redrawing an HTML Web page, thereby enabling you to show state in a single-page application.

Prior to HTML5, the browser support for history-related APIs provided limited functionality. You could find the number of items in the browser history, move forward and backward, and move several links backward, as shown here:

```
console.log(history.length);
console.log(history.forward());
console.log(history.back());
console.log(history.go(-2));
Several new APIs are available, as shown here:
history.pushState(data, title, url);
history.replaceState(data, title, url);
```

The parameters in the `history.pushState()` method are as follows:

`data` is some type of structured data, assigned to the history item
`title` is the name of the item in the history drop-down that is displayed by the browser's back and forward buttons
`url` is the (optional) URL that is displayed in the address bar

The parameters in the `history.replaceState()` method are the same as the `history.pushState()` method, except that the former updates information that is already in the browser's history.

In addition, there is the new `popstate` event, which occurs when users view their browser history. You can use it in the following manner:

```
window.addEventListener("popstate", function(event) {
  // do something here
});
```

Keep in mind that different browsers implement HTML5 browser history in different ways, so the following JavaScript toolkit is useful:

https://github.com/balupton/History.js/

The History.js toolkit supports jQuery, MooTools, and Prototype, and in HTML5 browsers you can modify the URL directly without resorting to hashes.

INTRODUCTION TO WEBGL

WebGL is an implementation of OpenGL (a cross-platform 3D drawing standard created in 1992) that provides JavaScript bindings for OpenGL ES 2 in order to access OpenGL functionality. WebGL is moving toward standardization, and the process involves the Khronos Group (which is responsible for OpenGL) and browser vendors.

WebGL has a pipeline-oriented architecture, along with "fragment shaders" for textures and "vertex shaders" for managing vertex buffers. The programming language is GLSL (GL Shading Language) that is similar to the C programming language.

Currently you need to invoke the `getContext()` method with vendor prefixes, such as `moz-webgl` and `webkit-3d`, in order to obtain a 3D context. Although WebGL is arguably more complicated than drawing lines, rectangles, and shapes in HTML5 Canvas, WebGL enables you to render much richer graphics and animation effects.

You can determine whether or not your machine supports WebGL by navigating to this Web site:

http://get.webgl.org/

There are several JavaScript-based toolkits available that provide a layer of abstraction on top of OpenGL APIs that "shield" you from having to learn the lower level details, including the following toolkits:

- Three.js
- PhiloGL
- SceneJS

As this book goes to print, Three.js has the largest number of users on its forum (more than the next two combined), which is a reasonable indicator of the level of activity surrounding Three.js. However, keep in mind that the pace of development of Three.js also means that APIs change frequently, and backward compatibility might not be available. In addition, do not discount the value of other toolkits; it's certainly possible that they provide functionality that is closer to your needs.

One unfortunate fact is that currently there is virtually no support for WebGL on mobile devices, but that is destined to change (hopefully soon!).

Three.js

The Three.js open source project is a JavaScript-based toolkit that provides a layer of abstraction on top of OpenGL, and you can download the Three.js source code here:

https://github.com/mrdoob/three.js/
http://learningthreejs.com/blog/2012/01/17/dom-events-in-3d-space/

Currently the Three.js documentation is sparse, but hopefully that will improve over time. You can find some code samples by performing an Internet search, and if you encounter difficulties, *www.stackoverflow.com* is a very good place to search for answers to your questions.

In brief, there are three objects that you must always create in Three.js in order to render graphics objects in an HTML page with Three.js:

1. A scene (to put things that you want people to see)
2. A camera (which can be moved around)
3. A renderer (a `<canvas>`, `<svg>`, or WebGL renderer).

After creating a camera, you can move it around to see the objects in the scene from different points of view.

Three.js also supports three different renderers for creating graphics effects using HTML5 Canvas, WebGL, and SVG.

Some people might find Three.js straightforward and intuitive, and others might experience a steeper learning curve (it depends on your background).

The following online tool shows you the results of changing the attributes of a camera (rotation and position) and the position of the light source, along with the coordinates of two cubes:

http://hotblocks.nl/tests/three/cubes.html

Although Three.js provides built-in support only for cubes, cylinders, and spheres, which is not as extensive as other 2D toolkits, you can create very rich 3D visual effects with Three.js. You can also create 3D animation effects in Three.js, as shown later in this section.

Another interesting project is ThreeJS Boilerplate, whose goal is to apply the same principles of HTML5 BoilerPlate to HTML Web pages that use Three.js. It's available for download here:

https://github.com/jeromeetienne/threejsboilerplate

Rendering a Sphere and a Cylinder using a WebGL Renderer

The example in this section is in lieu of the traditional "Hello World" application, and the code illustrates the basic sequence of steps that you need to perform in Web pages that use Three.js.

Listing 8.3 displays the contents of `Sphere1Cylinder1.html`, which illustrates how to render a sphere and a cylinder in Three.js.

LISTING 8.3 Sphere1Cylinder1.html

```
<!DOCTYPE html>
<html lang="en">
 <head>
  <meta charset="utf-8" />
  <title>Sphere and Cylinder</title>
  <script src="Three45.js">
  </script>

<script>
  function draw() {
      var renderer = new THREE.WebGLRenderer();
      renderer.setSize(window.innerWidth, window.innerHeight);
      document.body.appendChild(renderer.domElement);

      // create a camera
```

```
     var camera = new THREE.PerspectiveCamera(
                    45,
                    window.innerWidth/window.innerHeight,
                    1, 1000);

     camera.position.z = 800;

     // create a scene
     var scene = new THREE.Scene();

     // create a sphere
     var sphere = new THREE.Mesh(
               new THREE.SphereGeometry(100, 20, 20),
             new THREE.MeshLambertMaterial({color: 0x0000ff}));

     sphere.overdraw = true;
     sphere.scale.y = 0.5;
     scene.add(sphere);

     var cylinder = new THREE.Mesh(
               new THREE.CylinderGeometry(
                              100,100,200,16,4,false),
               new THREE.MeshLambertMaterial(
                              {color: 0x2D303D,
                               wireframe: true,
                               shading: THREE.FlatShading})
               );

     scene.add(cylinder);

     // add some ambient lighting
     var ambientLight = new THREE.AmbientLight(0x555555);
     scene.add(ambientLight);

     // add a directional light source
     var directionalLight = new THREE.DirectionalLight(0xffffff);
     directionalLight.position.set(1, 1, 1).normalize();
     scene.add(directionalLight);

     renderer.render(scene, camera);
   }
  </script>
 </head>

<body onload="draw()">
</body>
</html>
```

Listing 8.3 starts by referencing the JavaScript file Three45.js (other versions might not work with this code sample), followed by the JavaScript draw() function that creates a renderer, a camera, and a scene (which you know are the minimum requirements for a Web page that uses Three.js).

The next portion of this function creates a sphere in Three.js by specifying a SphereGeometry, as shown here:

```
var sphere = new THREE.Mesh(
            new THREE.SphereGeometry(100, 20, 20),
            new THREE.MeshLambertMaterial({color: 0x0000ff}));
```

Notice how easily you can create a sphere in Three.js by means of the built-in functionality that is show in the preceding code block (the WebGL code would be significantly more complicated).

The second object in Listing 8.3 is a cylinder, which you can create in Three.js by specifying a `CylinderGeometry` and a `MeshLambertMaterial`, as shown here:

```
var cylinder = new THREE.Mesh(
            new THREE.CylinderGeometry(
                            100,100,200,16,4,false),
            new THREE.MeshLambertMaterial(
                            {color: 0x2D303D,
                             wireframe: true,
                             shading: THREE.FlatShading})
            );
```

Next, the sphere and the cylinder are appended to the scene, along with a newly created light source, and then the objects are rendered. The preceding description is admittedly sparse, but as you can see, Three.js makes it very easy to create various geometric shapes by hiding the tedious underlying details.

Figure 8.3 displays the graphics image that is rendered by the code in Listing 8.3.

THE TQUERY JQUERY PLUGIN FOR THREE.JS

The tQuery jQuery plugin is a plugin that provides a layer of abstraction over the Three.js toolkit, and its homepage is here:

http://jeromeetienne.github.com/tquery/

Listing 8.4 displays the contents of `Torus1.html` that illustrates the ease with which you can render a torus using a minimal amount of `tquery` code.

FIGURE 8.3 Rendering a sphere and a cylinder

LISTING 8.4 TORUS1.HTML

```
<!doctype html>
<html>
 <head>
   <meta charset="utf-8" />
   <title>Minimal tQuery Page</title>
   <script src="./tquery-all.js"></script>
 <head>

 <body>
  <script>
    var world  = tQuery.createWorld().boilerplate().start();
    var object = tQuery.createTorus().addTo(world);
  </script>
 </body>
</html>
```

As you can see, Listing 8.4 consists of very basic HTML markup, a reference to the JavaScript file `tquery-all.js`, and a mere *two lines* of JavaScript code in a `<script>` element that renders a torus (could the code be any simpler than this?)

Figure 8.4 displays the torus that is rendered by the code in Listing 8.4.

OTHER GRAPHICS TOOLKITS

CSG (Constructive Solid Geometry) is an open source toolkit that provides a layer of functionality on top of WebGL. Its homepage is here:

https://github.com/evanw/csg.js/

CAAT (Canvas Advanced Animation Toolkit) is an open source project. You can find demos and tutorials on the CAAT homepage:

http://labs.hyperandroid.com/static/caat/

You can download the code from GitHub:

https://github.com/hyperandroid/CAAT-Samples

PERFORMANCE, DEBUGGING, AND TESTING TOOLS

Several excellent performance and debugging tools are available, and this section briefly mentions several of these tools:

- Blaze (mobile Web sites)
- Chrome PageSpeed (mobile Web sites)
- Chrome Speed Tracer
- PageSpeed Insights

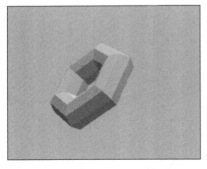

FIGURE 8.4 Rendering a torus with tQuery

- WEINRE
- YSlow

Before we discuss these tools, remember that the code samples in this book are for `WebKit`-based browsers, and in case you haven't already done so, you ought to familiarize yourself with the Web Inspector, which is built into Chrome and Safari. Whenever you navigate to a Web page, right click on that Web page and you can view details about the Web page that you have launched.

For example, Figure 8.5 shows you what you will see if you launch the HTML5 Web page `HTML5Video1.html` in a Chrome browser, right click on the page, and then click on "Resources."

The Web Inspector is a very useful tool, and it's well worth your time familiarizing yourself with its features. A Wiki page with useful information about Web Inspector is here:

http://trac.webkit.org/wiki/WebInspector

Blaze

Blaze provides test results for the performance of a mobile Web site, which includes overall load time as well as load times for individual pages. Blaze supports multiple mobile devices, including iPhone, iPad 2 (but not iPad 3), and devices with Android 2.2/2.3/3.0 (but no support yet for Android ICS).

Navigate to the following URL and follow the instructions:

http://www.blaze.io/mobile/

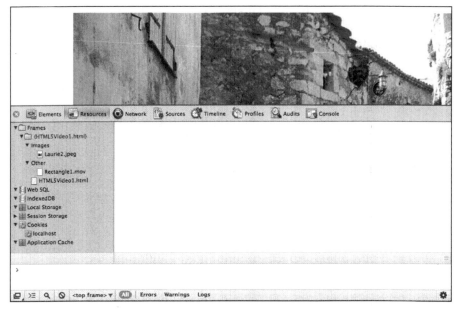

FIGURE 8.5 An example of Chrome's Web Inspector

Google PageSpeed

Google PageSpeed tests load time on desktop browsers, and there is also a Web version of Google PageSpeed for analyzing mobile performance. Google PageSpeed ranks a page between 1 and 100, and also provides suggestions for improving the performance of a mobile Web site:

http://pagespeed.googlelabs.com/

Chrome Speed Tracer

Chrome Speed Tracer is an open source project that assists you in identifying performance bottlenecks in your Web applications. Its homepage is here:

https://developers.google.com/web-toolkit/speedtracer/

Speed Tracer performs low-level instrumentation; after performing an analysis, the results are displayed in a visually oriented fashion. Speed Tracer is currently available as a Chrome extension and works on its supported platforms (Windows and Linux).

PageSpeed Insights

PageSpeed Insights is actually a "family" of tools for optimizing the performance of Web pages. Its homepage is here:

https://developers.google.com/speed/pagespeed/insights

The PageSpeed available tools are:

* PageSpeed browser extensions
* PageSpeed Insight
* The `mod_pagespeed` Apache module
* PageSpeed service

The PageSpeed browser extensions are available for Chrome and Firefox, and help you improve the performance of your Web pages.

PageSpeed Insights is a Web-based tool that analyzes pages in any browser, without downloading an extension. The `mod_pagespeed` Apache module automatically rewrites pages and resources to improve their performance. Finally, PageSpeed service is an online service that speeds up loading of your Web pages.

WEINRE

WEINRE (pronounced "winery") is an excellent debugging tool that uses the same UI display as Chrome's Web Inspector. Its homepage is here:

http://phonegap.github.com/weinre/

WEINRE supports remote debugging, which means that you can see Web pages on mobile devices. You can find YouTube videos, documentation, and discussion groups regarding WEINRE here:

http://www.youtube.com/results?search_query=weinre
http://callback.github.com/callback-weinre
http://groups.google.com/group/weinre

Firebug for Firefox

Firebug is a debugging tool that is an addon for Firefox. You can install Firebug here:

https://addons.mozilla.org/en-US/firefox/addon/firebug/

There are also simulation tools available, such as the one by Remy Sharp that allows you to simulate motion events on mobile devices:

http://remote-tilt.com/

You can use this tool by including one line of JavaScript in your Web pages, after which a pop-up window will appear that enables you to simulate various motion events.

Unfortunately, additional discussion about these tools is beyond the primary scope of this book, but it's definitely worth learning at least one of them, which will provide you with knowledge that you can use for debugging purposes outside of the code samples this book.

jsconsole

jsconsole is a JavaScript and CoffeeScript web console that is useful for debugging purposes. This tool (created by Remy Sharp) is available for download here:

https://github.com/remy/jsconsole

You can see examples of the functionality of jsconsole on this Web site:

http://jsconsole.com/

Socketbug

Socketbug is a tool created by Peter Schmalfeldt that helps you debug mobile applications:

http://socketbug.com/

SocketBug supports iOS Safari, Android *Webkit*, and Palm WebOS, and you can use any modern browser as your debug console.

Adobe Edge Inspect

Adobe Edge Inspect (formerly called Adobe Shadow) is a mobile debugging tool by Adobe:

http://html.adobe.com/edge/inspect/

Adobe Edge Inspect provides a way to test your Web sites on multiple devices simultaneously, which is also appealing if you are interested in responsive design. Adobe Edge Inspect uses WEINRE in order to perform remote DOM inspection on devices, and it currently supports Mac (OS X 10.6 and 10.7) and Windows 7. A six-minute video about Adobe Edge Inspect is here:

https://www.youtube.com/watch?v=SyzZHS-1fPE

WebKit Remote Debugging

Another very useful debugging tool is `WebKit` Remote Debugging, which has been available since 2011, and it is also shipping in iOS and Android. You can download the code from GitHub here:

http://code.google.com/p/chromedevtools/wiki/WebKitProtocol

Additional details regarding `WebKit` Remote Debugging are available here:

http://www.webkit.org/blog/1875/announcing-remote-debugging-protocol-v1-0/

SUMMARY

This chapter start with an introduction to Microformats. Next you saw code samples that showed you how to work with DnD and HTML5 File APIs. You also learned about WebGL and toolkits (such as Three.js and tQuery) that provide a layer of abstraction on top of WebGL. Finally, you learned about various performance-related toolkits that are available.

HTML5 MOBILE APPS ON ANDROID AND IOS

T his chapter shows you how to create HTML5-based hybrid mobile applications for Android and iOS. The code samples in this chapter contain HTML5 and various combinations of HTML5, CSS3, and SVG.

The first part of this chapter provides an overview of how to develop hybrid Android applications. The code samples in this section use the same code that you have seen in earlier chapters, and show you how to create the hybrid Android mobile applications that will enable you to create the same screenshots. If you feel ambitious, you can create Android-based mobile applications for all the code samples in this book!

The second part of this chapter contains Android-based code samples that show you how to combine native Android applications with CSS3, SVG, and HTML5 Canvas. This section contains an example of rendering a mouse-enabled multi-line graph whose values can be updated whenever users click on the button that is rendered underneath the line graph. Keep in mind that the discussion following the code samples moves quickly because the HTML Web pages contain simple markup, the CSS3 selectors contain code that you have seen in earlier chapters, and the SVG shapes are discussed in Chapter 4.

The third part of this chapter provides a quick overview of Apache Cordova, formerly known as PhoneGap, which is a popular cross-platform toolkit for developing mobile applications. In 2011, Adobe acquired Nitobi, the company that created PhoneGap, and shortly thereafter Adobe open sourced PhoneGap. This section explains what PhoneGap can do, and also some toolkits that you can use with PhoneGap. You will learn how to create a PhoneGap-based Android application that renders CSS3-based animation effects, and you can deploy this mobile application to Android-based mobile devices that support Android ICS or higher. Keep in mind that the term "PhoneGap" is used in this chapter (and sometimes even by Adobe) to refer to Cordova because the name change is very recent, and there is a huge installed code base that still refers to Cordova as PhoneGap.

The final part of this chapter shows you some of the functionality of Xcode 4.3, and you will see the steps for creating a "Hello World" mobile application for iOS devices. You will also learn how to create hybrid iOS-based mobile applications using the PhoneGap plugin for Xcode.

As you will see in this chapter, PhoneGap allows you to create mobile applications using HTML, CSS, and JavaScript, and you can deploy those mobile applications to numerous platforms, including Android, iOS, Black-Berry and Windows Mobile. You can also create mobile applications that combine PhoneGap with Sencha Touch (another popular framework), but due to space limitations, Sencha Touch is not discussed in this chapter.

If you are unfamiliar with any of the mobile platforms in this chapter, you can still work through the examples because they consist of HTML5-based code, and the sequence of steps for creating HTML5-based mobile applications on a mobile platform is essentially independent of the actual code.

HTML5/CSS3 AND ANDROID APPLICATIONS

If you are unfamiliar with Android, the appendix contains a concise overview of the Android-specific concepts in the code samples in this chapter. You can refer to the appropriate section whenever you encounter an Android concept that is not clear to you.

The code sample in this section shows you how to launch an HTML5 Web page (which also references a CSS3 stylesheet) inside an Android application. The key idea consists of three steps:

1. Modify the Android `Activity` class to instantiate an Android `WebView` class, along with some JavaScript-related settings
2. Reference an HTML5 Web page that is in the `assets/www` subdirectory of the Android project
3. Copy the HTML5 Web page, CSS stylesheets, and JavaScript files into the `assets/www` subdirectory of the Android project

In Step 3 above, you will probably create a hierarchical set of directories that contain files that are of the same type (HTML, CSS, or JavaScript), in much the same way that you organize your files in a Web application.

Now launch Eclipse and create an Android project called "AndroidCSS3," making sure that you select Android version 3.1 or higher, which is necessary in order to render CSS3-based effects.

After you have created the project, let's take a look at four files that contain the custom code for this Android mobile application. Listing 9.1, 9.2, and 9.3 display the contents of the project files `main.xml`, `AndroidCSS3.html`, and `AndroidCSS3Activity.java`.

LISTING 9.1: main.xml

```
<?xml version="1.0" encoding="utf-8"?>
<LinearLayout   xmlns:android="http://schemas.android.com/apk/res/
android"
    android:orientation="vertical"
    android:layout_width="fill_parent"
    android:layout_height="fill_parent">
  <WebView android:id="@+id/webview"
            android:layout_width="fill_parent"
            android:layout_height="fill_parent">
  </WebView>
</LinearLayout>
```

Listing 9.1 specifies a `LinearLayout` that contains an Android `Web-View` that will occupy the entire screen of the mobile device. This is the behavior that we want to see, because Android default browser is rendered inside the Android `WebView`.

LISTING 9.2: AndroidCSS3.html

```
<!doctype html>
<head>
  <title>CSS Radial Gradient Example</title>
  <link href="AndroidCSS3.css" rel="stylesheet">
</head>

<body>
 <div id="outer">
  <div id="radial1">Text1</div>
  <div id="radial2">Text2</div>
  <div id="radial3">Text3</div>
  <div id="radial4">Text4</div>
 </div>
</body>
</html>
```

Listing 9.2 is a straightforward HTML Web page that references a CSS stylesheet `AndroidCSS3.css` (that is available on the DVD), along with an HTML `<div>` element (whose `id` attribute has value `outer`) that serves as a "container" for four more HTML `<div>` elements.

The CSS stylesheet `AndroidCSS3.css` contains a CSS selector for styling the HTML `<div>` element whose id has value `outer`, followed by four CSS selectors `radial1`, `radial2`, `radial3`, and `radial4` that are used to style the corresponding HTML `<div>` elements in Listing 9.2. The contents of these selectors ought to be very familiar (you can review the material for CSS3 gradients in an earlier chapter), so we will not cover their contents in this section.

LISTING 9.3: AndroidCSS3Activity.java

```
package com.iquarkt.css3;

import android.app.Activity;
import android.os.Bundle;
```

```
import android.webkit.WebChromeClient;
import android.webkit.WebSettings;
import android.webkit.WebView;
import android.webkit.WebViewClient;

public class AndroidCSS3Activity extends Activity
{
    /** Called when the activity is first created. */
    @Override
    public void onCreate(Bundle savedInstanceState)
    {
        super.onCreate(savedInstanceState);
        setContentView(R.layout.main);

        // Get a reference to the declared WebView holder
        WebView webview = (WebView) this.findViewById(R.id.webview);

        // Get the settings
        WebSettings webSettings = webview.getSettings();

        // Enable Javascript for interaction
        webSettings.setJavaScriptEnabled(true);

        // Make the zoom controls visible
        webSettings.setBuiltInZoomControls(true);

        // Allow for touching selecting/deselecting data series
        webview.requestFocusFromTouch();

        // Set the client
        webview.setWebViewClient(new WebViewClient());
        webview.setWebChromeClient(new WebChromeClient());

        // Load the URL
        webview.loadUrl("file:///android_asset/AndroidCSS3.html");
    }
}
```

Listing 9.3 defines a Java class `AndroidCSS3Activity` that extends the standard Android `Activity` class. This class contains the `onCreate()` method that "points" to the XML document `main.xml` (displayed in Listing 9.2) so that we can get a reference to its `WebView` child element via `R.id.webview` (which is the reference to the `WebView` element in Listing 9.2), as shown here:

```
WebView webview = (WebView) this.findViewById(R.id.webview);
```

Next, the `webSettings` instance of the `WebSettings` class enables us to set various properties, as shown in the commented lines of code in Listing 9.4.

The final line of code loads the contents of the HTML Web page `AndroidCSS3.html` (which is in the assets/www subdirectory), as shown here:

```
webview.loadUrl("file:///android_asset/AndroidCSS3.html");
```

Figure 9.1 displays a CSS3-based Android application on an Asus Prime tablet with Android ICS.

SVG AND ANDROID APPLICATIONS

The example in this section shows you how to create an Android mobile application that renders SVG code that is embedded in an HTML5 Web page. Now launch Eclipse and create an Android project called "AndroidSVG1," making sure that you select Android version 3.1 or higher, which is necessary in order to render SVG elements.

The example in the previous section contains four custom files, whereas the Android/SVG example in this section contains two files with custom code: the HTML5 Web page `AndroidSVG1.html` in Listing 9.4 and the Java class `AndroidSVG1.java`, which available on the DVD.

LISTING 9.4: AndroidSVG1.html

```
<!DOCTYPE html>
<html>
  <body>
    <h1>HTML5/SVG Example</h1>
    <svg>
      <ellipse cx="300" cy="50" rx="80" ry="40"
               fill="#ff0" stroke-dasharray="8 4 8 1"
               style="stroke:red;stroke-width:4;"/>

      <line x1="100" y1="20" x2="300" y2="350"
            stroke-dasharray="8 4 8 1"
            style="stroke:red;stroke-width:8;"/>
```

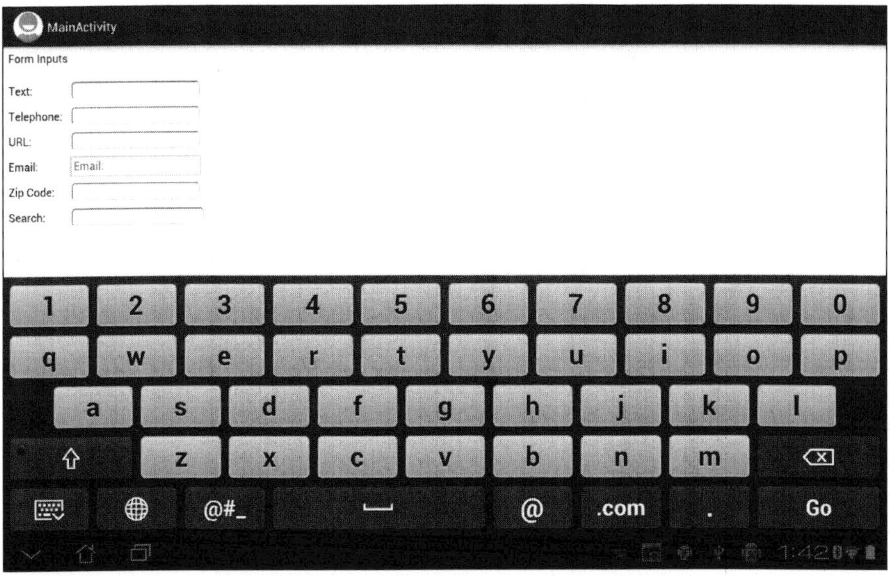

FIGURE 9.1 A CSS3-based 3D cube on an Asus Prime tablet with Android ICS

```
      <g transform="translate(20,20)">
        <path
           d="M0,0 C200,150 400,300 20,250"
           fill="#f00"
           stroke-dasharray="4 4 4 4"
           style="stroke:blue;stroke-width:4;"/>
      </g>

      <g transform="translate(200,50)">
        <path
           d="M200,150 C0,0 400,300 20,250"
           fill="#00f"
           stroke-dasharray="12 12 12 12"
           style="stroke:blue;stroke-width:4;"/>
      </g>
    </svg>
  </body>
</html>
```

Listing 9.4 is an HTML Web page that contains an SVG document with the definitions for an ellipse, a line segment, and two cubic Bezier curves. Appendix A contains examples of these 2D shapes (among others), and you can review the appropriate material if you need to refresh your memory.

The Java class `AndroidSVG1Activity.java` is omitted, but its contents are very similar to Listing 9.3, and the complete source code is available on the DVD.

Figure 9.2 displays an SVG -based Android application on an Asus Prime tablet with Android ICS.

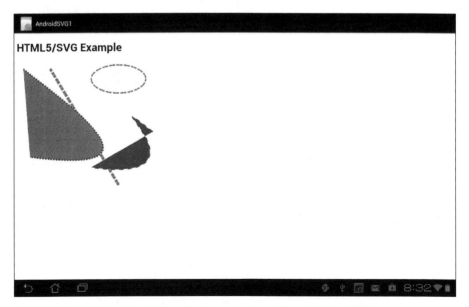

FIGURE 9.2 An SVG-based Android application on an Asus tablet with Android ICS

HTML5 CANVAS AND ANDROID APPLICATIONS

In addition to rendering CSS3-based effects and SVG documents, you can also render Canvas-based 2D shapes in an Android application. Launch Eclipse and create an Android project called "AndroidCanvas1," making sure that you select Android version 3.1 or higher, which is necessary in order to render SVG elements.

The example in this section contains one custom file called `AndroidCanvas1.html`, which is displayed in Listing 9.5.

LISTING 9.5: AndroidCanvas1.html

```
<!DOCTYPE html>
<html lang="en">
<head>
<meta charset="utf-8">
<title>Android Canvas</title>

<script>
 function draw() {
    var basePointX  = 10;
    var basePointY  = 80;
    var currentX    = 0;
    var currentY    = 0;
    var startAngle  = 0;
    var endAngle    = 0;
    var radius      = 120;
    var lineLength  = 200;
    var lineWidth   = 1;
    var lineCount   = 200;
    var lineColor   = "";

    var hexArray    = new Array('0','1','2','3','4','5','6','7',
                                '8','9','a','b','c','d','e','f');

    var can = document.getElementById('canvas1');
    var ctx = can.getContext('2d');

    // render a text string...
    ctx.font = "bold 26px helvetica, arial, sans-serif";
    ctx.shadowColor = "#333333";
    ctx.shadowOffsetX = 2;
    ctx.shadowOffsetY = 2;
    ctx.shadowBlur = 2;
    ctx.fillStyle = 'red';
    ctx.fillText("HTML5 Canvas/Android", 0, 30);

    for(var r=0; r<lineCount; r++) {
        currentX = basePointX+r;
        currentY = basePointY+r;
        startAngle = (360-r/2)*Math.PI/180;
        endAngle   = (360+r/2)*Math.PI/180;

        // render the first line segment...
        lineColor = '#' + hexArray[r%16] + '00';
```

```
        ctx.strokeStyle = lineColor;
        ctx.lineWidth   = lineWidth;

        ctx.beginPath();
        ctx.moveTo(currentX, currentY+2*r);
        ctx.lineTo(currentX+lineLength, currentY+2*r);
        ctx.closePath();
        ctx.stroke();
        ctx.fill();

        // render the second line segment...
        lineColor = '#' + '0' + hexArray[r%16] + '0';
        ctx.beginPath();
        ctx.moveTo(currentX, currentY);
        ctx.lineTo(currentX+lineLength, currentY);
        ctx.closePath();
        ctx.stroke();
        ctx.fill();

        // render the arc...
        lineColor = '#' + '00'+ hexArray[(2*r)%16];
        ctx.beginPath();
        ctx.fillStyle = lineColor;
        ctx.moveTo(currentX, currentY);
        ctx.arc(currentX, currentY, radius,
                startAngle, endAngle, false);
        ctx.closePath();
        ctx.stroke();
        ctx.fill();
    }
}
</script>
</head>

<body onload="draw()">
  <canvas id="canvas1" width="300px" height="200px"></canvas>
</body>
<html>
```

Listing 9.5 contains some boilerplate HTML markup and a JavaScript function draw() that is executed when the Web page is loaded into the Android browser. The draw() function contains JavaScript code that draws a set of line segments and arcs into the HTML5 <canvas> element whose id attribute has value canvas1. You can review the code samples in Chapter 11 that have similar functionality if you don't remember the details of the syntax of this JavaScript code.

Figure 9.3 displays a Canvas-based Android application on an Asus Prime tablet with Android ICS.

ANDROID AND HTML5 CANVAS MULTI-LINE GRAPHS

Although Android does not have built-in support for rendering charts and graphs, you can create them using Canvas-based code that is very similar to the code in the previous section.

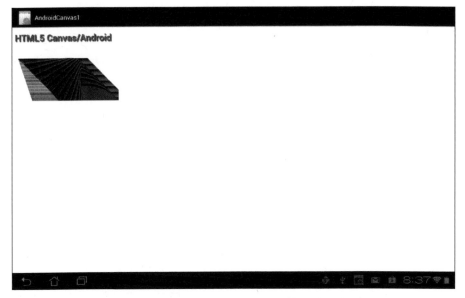

FIGURE 9.3 A Canvas-based Android application on an Asus tablet with Android ICS

Launch Eclipse and create an Android project called "AndroidCanvasMultiLine2," making sure that you select Android version 3.1 or higher. Listing 9.6 displays portions of the HTML5 Web page `AndroidCanvasMultiLine2.html` that contains JavaScript code for rendering multiple line graphs using HTML5 Canvas.

LISTING 9.6: AndroidCanvasMultiLine2.html

```
<!DOCTYPE html>
<html lang="en">
 <head>
  <meta charset="utf-8" />
  <title>HTML5 Canvas Line Graphs</title>

  <script>
    // JavaScript variables omitted for brevity
    var lineCount    = 3;
    var barHeights   = new Array(barCount);
    var barHeights2  = new Array(barCount);
    var barHeights3  = new Array(barCount);
    var currHeights  = new Array(barCount);
    var multiLines   = new Array(lineCount);
    var fillColors   = new Array("#F00", "#FF0", "#0F0", "#00F");
    var elem, context, gradient1;

    function drawGraph() {
        drawGraph2();
    }

    function randomBarValues() {
        for(var i=0; i<barCount; i++) {
```

```
            barHeight = maxHeight*Math.random();
            barHeights[i] = barHeight;

            barHeight = maxHeight*Math.random();
            barHeights2[i] = barHeight;

            barHeight = maxHeight*Math.random();
            barHeights3[i] = barHeight;
        }

        multiLines[0] = barHeights;
        multiLines[1] = barHeights2;
        multiLines[2] = barHeights3;
    }

    function drawGraph2() {
        // clear the canvas before drawing new set of rectangles
        context.clearRect(0, 0, elem.width, elem.height);

        randomBarValues();
        drawAndLabelAxes();
        drawElements();
    }

    function drawElements() {
        for(var h=0; h<multiLines.length; h++) {
            currHeights = multiLines[h];

            currentX = leftBorder;
          //currentY = maxHeight-barHeights[0];
            currentY = maxHeight-currHeights[0];

            // draw line segments...
            for(var i=0; i<barCount; i++) {
                context.beginPath();
                context.moveTo(currentX, currentY);
                currentX = leftBorder+i*barWidth;
              //currentY = maxHeight-barHeights[i];
                currentY = maxHeight-currHeights[i];

                context.shadowColor   = "rgba(100,100,100,.5)";
                context.shadowOffsetX = 3;
                context.shadowOffsetY = 3;
                context.shadowBlur    = 5;

                context.lineWidth   = 4;
                context.strokeStyle = fillColors[i%4];
                context.lineCap     = "miter"; // "round";

                context.lineTo(currentX, currentY);
                context.stroke();
            }
        }

        drawBarText();
    }
```

```
    </script>
  </head>

<body onload="drawGraph();">
  <header>
    <h1>HTML5 Canvas Line Graphs</h1>
  </header>

  <div>
    <canvas id="myCanvas" width="500" height="300">No support for
Canvas
    </canvas>
  </div>

  <input type="button" onclick="drawGraph();return false"
       value="Update Graph Values" />
</body>
</html>
```

The JavaScript function `drawGraph()` in Listing 9.6 is invoked when the HTML5 Web page is loaded, and it invokes JavaScript functions to calculate the vertices for three separate line graphs, render labels for the graphs, and then render the three line graphs.

The last step involves a nested loop, where the outer loop iterates through the elements of the array `multiLines`, and the inner loop renders one line graph with every iteration through the outer loop.

Figure 9.4 displays a Canvas-based multi-line graph Android application on a Nexus S 4G with Android ICS.

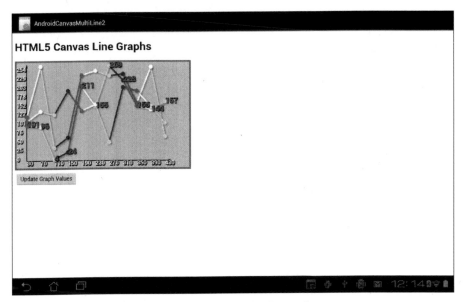

FIGURE 9.4 A Canvas-based multi-line graph on an Android smartphone

OTHER CODE SAMPLES

The Android project HTML5CanvasBBall2 contains the HTML5 Web page `HTML5CanvasBBall2.html` that contains JavaScript code for creating a bouncing ball effect in HTML5 Canvas.

The next portion of this chapter delves into PhoneGap, which is a toolkit that automatically creates the lower level "scaffolding" that you performed manually in the previous part of this chapter. You will get instructions for installing the PhoneGap plugin for Eclipse to create Android mobile applications, and later in this chapter you will learn how to install the PhoneGap plugin for Xcode in order to create HTML5-based mobile applications for iOS mobile devices.

WHAT IS PHONEGAP?

PhoneGap is an open source device agnostic mobile application development tool that enables you to create cross-platform mobile applications using CSS, HTML, and JavaScript, and its homepage is here:

http://phonegap.com

The PhoneGap homepage provides documentation, code samples, and a download link for the PhoneGap distribution.

PhoneGap provides support for touch events, event listeners, rendering images, database access, different file formats (XML and JSON), and Web services. PhoneGap enables you to create HTML-based mobile application for Android, Blackberry, iPhone, Palm, Symbian, and Windows Mobile. Note that if you want to develop iPhone applications, you must have a Macbook or some other Mac-based machine, along with other dependencies that are discussed later in this chapter.

How Does PhoneGap Work?

PhoneGap mobile applications involve a Web view that is embedded in a native "shell," and your custom code runs in the Web view. In addition, PhoneGap provides a JavaScript API for accessing native features of a mobile device, and your code can use PhoneGap in order to access those native features. For example, PhoneGap contains JavaScript APIs for accessing accelerometer, camera, compass, contacts, device information, events, geolocation, media, notification, and storage.

Keep in mind that PhoneGap does not provide HTML UI elements, so if you need this functionality in your mobile applications, you can add other toolkits and frameworks, such as jQuery Mobile, Sencha Touch, or Appcelerator.

Now that you have a basic understanding of the capabilities of PhoneGap, install Cordova 2.1 (which was released as this book goes to print) for Xcode and Eclipse by selecting the Android link and the iOS link on this Web page and then following the instructions:

http://docs.phonegap.com/en/2.1.0/guide_getting-started_index.md.html

In case you prefer to compile your mobile applications in the "cloud," Adobe provides a Web site for this purpose:

https://build.phonegap.com/

If you have completed the installation of the PhoneGap plugin for Eclipse, you are ready to create a PhoneGap application for Android, which is the topic of the next section.

CREATING ANDROID APPS WITH THE PHONEGAP PLUGIN

Create an Android project in Eclipse by clicking on the icon for the PhoneGap plugin and then (for the purposes of this example) specify "PGJQM1" for the Project Name, check the checkbox for including the jQuery Mobile files, select the Android version that your Android device supports, and then enter com.iquarkt.phonegap (or some other suitable string) as the package name.

Click the "Finish" button and after the project has been created, navigate to the assets/www subdirectory of the newly created Android project, and you will find the following files (version numbers might be different when this book goes to print):

```
index.html
cordova-1.6.0.js
```

There is also a generated Java file PhoneGap1Activity.java, whose contents are displayed in Listing 9.7.

LISTING 9.7 PHONEGAP1ACTIVITY.JAVA
```java
package com.iquarkt.phonegap;

import com.phonegap.*;
import android.os.Bundle;

public class PhoneGap1Activity extends Activity
{
    /** Called when the activity is first created. */
    @Override
    public void onCreate(Bundle savedInstanceState)
    {
      super.onCreate(savedInstanceState); setContentView(R.layout.main);
        super.loadUrl("file:///android_asset/www/index.html");
    }
}
```

Listing 9.7 contains an onCreate() method that launches the HTML page index.html, as shown here:

```java
super.loadUrl("file:///android_asset/www/index.html");
```

The HTML page index.html is located in the assets/www subdirectory of the project, and its contents are displayed in Listing 9.8.

LISTING 9.8 index.html

```html
<!DOCTYPE HTML>
<html>
  <head>
  <meta charset="utf-8">
    <meta name="viewport" content="width=320; user-scalable=no" />
        <meta   http-equiv="Content-type"   content="text/html;
charset=utf-8">
    <title>PhoneGap</title>

    <link rel="stylesheet" href="master.css"
        type="text/css" media="screen"
        title="no title" charset="utf-8">
    <script src="phonegap-1.0.0.js"></script>
    <script src="main.js"></script>
  </head>

  <body onload="init();" id="stage" class="theme">
    <h1>Welcome to PhoneGap!</h1>
    <h2>this file is located at assets/www/index.html</h2>
    <div id="info">
        <h4>Platform: <span id="platform">  </span>,   Version:
<span id="version"> </span></h4>
        <h4>UUID: <span id="uuid">  </span>,    Name: <span
id="name"> </span></h4>
        <h4>Width: <span id="width">  </span>,   Height: <span
id="height"> 
                    </span>, Color Depth: <span id="colorDepth"></
span></h4>
      </div>

    <dl id="accel-data">
      <dt>X:</dt><dd id="x"> </dd>
      <dt>Y:</dt><dd id="y"> </dd>
      <dt>Z:</dt><dd id="z"> </dd>
    </dl>

      <a href="#" class="btn large" onclick="toggleAccel();">Toggle
Accelerometer</a>
        <a href="#"  class="btn  large"  onclick="getLocation();">Get
Location</a>
      <a href="tel://411" class="btn large">Call 411</a>
      <a href="#" class="btn large" onclick="beep();">Beep</a>
      <a href="#" class="btn large" onclick="vibrate();">Vibrate</a>
        <a href="#"  class="btn  large"  onclick="show_pic();">Get  a
Picture</a>
        <a href="#"  class="btn  large"  onclick="get_contacts();">Get
Phone's Contacts</a>
        <a href="#"  class="btn  large"  onclick="check_network();">Check
Network</a>

      <div id="viewport" class="viewport" style="display: none;">
```

```
    <img style="width:60px;height:60px" id="test_img" src="" />
  </div>
 </body>
</html>
```

The first portion of Listing 9.8 contains a `<script>` element that includes the JavaScript file `phonegap.js`, which defines the functions that constitute the core functionality of PhoneGap.

The second portion of Listing 9.8 displays the anchor elements that enable you to test media-related features of your phone, including accelerometer, geolocation, making phone calls (from inside the Android application) beep effects, vibration effects, and taking pictures with the camera on your smartphone or tablet.

Listing 9.9 displays the contents of the Javascript file `main.js` that contains selected portions of the JavaScript code that supports the functionality in the HTML5 Web pages `index.html`.

LISTING 9.9: MAIN.JS

```
var deviceInfo = function() {
    document.getElementById("platform").innerHTML = device.platform;
    document.getElementById("version").innerHTML = device.version;
    document.getElementById("uuid").innerHTML = device.uuid;
    document.getElementById("name").innerHTML = device.name;
    document.getElementById("width").innerHTML = screen.width;
    document.getElementById("height").innerHTML = screen.height;
    document.getElementById("colorDepth").innerHTML =
                                        screen.colorDepth;
};

// sections omitted for brevity
function dump_pic(data) {
    var viewport = document.getElementById('viewport');
    console.log(data);
    viewport.style.display = "";
    viewport.style.position = "absolute";
    viewport.style.top = "10px";
    viewport.style.left = "10px";
    document.getElementById("test_img").src =
                            "data:image/jpeg;base64," + data;
}

function fail(msg) {
    alert(msg);
}

function show_pic() {
    navigator.camera.getPicture(dump_pic, fail, {
        quality : 50
    });
}

// details omitted for brevity
```

The first part of Listing 9.9 contains the code for getting the data from the accelerometer of your Android device. The second part of Listing 9.9 shows you the JavaScript code for taking a picture from this Android application.

From your Android device, navigate to Run > Android application in order to launch this Android project and you will see something similar to Figure 9.5.

Figure 9.5 displays a set of menu items that enable you to access hardware-related functionality.

OTHER CODE SAMPLES

The Android project PhoneGapForm1 contains the HTML5 Web page `PhoneGapForm1.html` (which will actually be named `index.html` in your Android project) that illustrates how to create a form for various types of user input in PhoneGap, and the types of the input fields are such that the following occurs when users navigate to this form:

- Text input displays a standard keyboard
- Telephone input displays a telephone keypad
- URL input displays a URL keyboard
- E-mail input displays an e-mail keyboard
- Zipcode input displays a numeric keyboard

Working with HTML5, PhoneGap, and iOS

This section shows you how to create iOS mobile applications using PhoneGap, which is exactly the process that was used to create the iOS mobile applications in this book, whose screenshots on an iPad 3 are included in various chapters. Every iOS mobile application in this book was developed on a Macbook OS X 10.7.3 with Apple's Xcode 4.3.1 and PhoneGap.

Earlier in this chapter, you learned how to create Android applications in Eclipse, which is an IDE that runs on multiple OSes, but the situation is different for creating iOS applications (with or without PhoneGap).

First you need access to an Apple development machine (such as a Macbook, Mac Mini, or Mac Pro) with Apple's Xcode installed in order to create mobile applications for iOS mobile devices. If you register as a developer you can download it for free, or for $4.99 in the Apple iStore. Although this section use Xcode 4.3.1 (which requires OS X 10.7.3), it's possible to install use a lower version of Xcode (such as 3.2) with a lower version of OS X.

Second, you need to install the PhoneGap plugin for Xcode 4 by following the detailed instructions here (which contain a link for installing PhoneGap on Xcode 3 as well):

http://wiki.phonegap.com/w/page/39991939/Getting%20Started%20 with%20PhoneGap%20iOS%20using%20Xcode%204

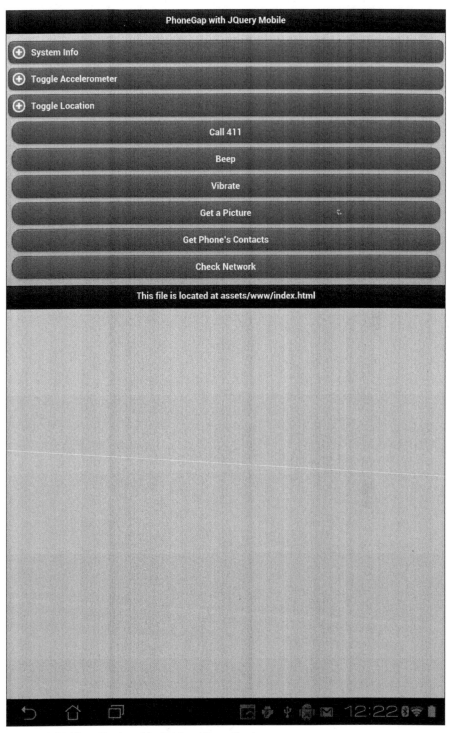

FIGURE 9.5 A PhoneGap-based Android mobile application

Third, you need to register as an Apple Developer (which costs $99 per year) *if you want to deploy your iOS mobile applications to iOS devices.* However, if you only plan to use the iOS Simulator, you can do so at no charge.

After you have set up a laptop with the required software, you will be ready to create an iOS mobile application with PhoneGap, which is the topic of the next section.

NOTE PhoneGap applications always have the same filename `index.html`, so in order to provide multiple PhoneGap project files in the same directory on the DVD, the HTML Web page `index.html` for each PhoneGap project is saved in a Web page whose name is the same as the project. For example, the HTML Web page `ThreeDCube1.html` on the DVD is actually the same as the generated Web page `index.html` that is specific to the PhoneGap project in the next section.

OTHER CODE SAMPLES

Create an Xcode application called `ThreeDCube1` by selecting the PhoneGap plugin (make sure that your filenames start with an alphabetic character or you will get errors when you attempt to compile and deploy your applications). Copy the CSS stylesheet `ThreeDCube1.css` into your project, and replace `index.html` with the HTML Web page `ThreeD-Cube1.html` in your project.

The process for creating the other iOS-based mobile applications in this chapter is identical to the process for the preceding iOS mobile application, so there is no need to include additional examples. However, it's worth your while to spend some time creating additional iOS mobile applications, which will increase your comfort level, and perhaps also motivate you to learn about other features of Xcode.

SUMMARY

This chapter showed you how to create hybrid Android mobile applications that contain HTML5, CSS3, and SVG. You created such mobile applications manually, which involved creating Android projects in Eclipse, and then modifying the contents of the Android `Activity` class and populating an assets subdirectory with HTML-related files.

Next, you learned how to use the PhoneGap Eclipse plugin, which simplifies the process of creating an Android project. You also saw how the Phon-eGap plugin creates a default page that allows you to use "live" features of your Android device.

JQUERY CONCEPTS

This chapter introduces you to jQuery and provides examples of using jQuery APIs to manipulate elements in HTML5 Web pages. jQuery is an extremely popular open source JavaScript-based toolkit that provides a layer of abstraction over JavaScript in order to facilitate the creation of HTML Web pages that run in multiple browsers.

The jQuery homepage provides a download link for the source code, along with documentation, developer resources, and other useful links:

http://jquery.org

jQuery is an open source JavaScript toolkit that enables you to write cross-browser and cross-platform JavaScript code for managing elements in an HTML Web page, which includes finding, creating, updating, and deleting not only elements, but also element attributes. This also includes the ability to add or remove style-related attributes of elements.

Some of the important and useful features of jQuery (in no particular order) include its support for cross-browser code, third-party jQuery plugins, themeable widgets, event handling, AJAX support, and simpler DOM traversal.

Note that Appendix A contains additional jQuery code samples.

USING JQUERY TO FIND ELEMENTS IN WEB PAGES

A key point to remember is that the "$" prefix is the jQuery function, which is a short-hand form of jQuery(). That means that the following two lines of code are the same:

```
var pElements1 = $("p");
var pElements2 = jQuery("p");
```

A third option is the use of window.jQuery, but this is less common than using jQuery or simply the "$" dollar sign.

One key point to remember is that a jQuery search actually returns a "result set," which is the set of elements that match the selection criteria. Each time a set of elements is returned, that set of elements can be passed to a second jQuery search, which in turn will return a set of elements matching the selection criteria of the second jQuery search. In fact, this process is called method chaining, and you "chain" together as many function invocations as you wish. Method chaining enables you to write very compact yet powerful code, as you will see in some examples in this chapter. As a preview, the following code snippet illustrates the use of jQuery method chaining:

```
$("ul li#item4").next().next().css({'font-size':24,
                           'background-color':'blue'});
```

As a simple example of how to use jQuery to select a set of elements in an HTML Web page, the following code snippet returns the set of `<p>` elements (if any) in an HTML Web page and assigns that set of elements to the JavaScript variable `pElements`:

```
var pElements = $("p");
```

The following code samples illustrate these and other jQuery concepts.

A "Hello World" Web Page with jQuery

The example in this section finds a *single* HTML `<p>` element and then changes its text. Later you will also see the modified code that enables you to manipulate an HTML Web page containing multiple HTML `<p>` elements.

Listing 10.1 displays the contents of `HelloWorld1.html` that illustrates how to add jQuery functionality to an HTML5 Web page that contains a single HTML `<p>` element.

NOTE Listing 10.1 contains `console.log()` that is available in WebKit-based browsers, but might not be available without some type of plugin or extension for other browsers.

LISTING 10.1: HelloWorld1.html

```
<!DOCTYPE html>
<html lang="en">
 <head>
 <meta charset="utf-8" />
 <title>Hello World</title>

 <script src="http://code.jquery.com/jquery-1.7.1.min.js">
 </script>
 </head>

 <body>
 <p id="Steve">Hello World From a Paragraph</p>

 <script>
```

```
$(document).ready(function(){
  // get the text in the <p> element
  var pText = $("p").text();
  console.log (pId+" says "+pText);

  // update the text in the <p> element
  $("p").text("Goodbye World From a Paragraph");
  pText = $("p").text();
  console.log(pId+" says "+pText);
});
    </script>
  </body>
</html>
```

Listing 10.1 references a required jQuery file with this code snippet:

```
<script src="http://code.jquery.com/jquery-1.7.1.min.js">
</script>
```

Notice that the first HTML <script> element in the HTML <body> element starts with this line:

```
$(document).ready(function(){
  // do something here
});
```

The preceding construct ensures that the DOM has been loaded into memory, so it's safe to access and manipulate DOM elements.

You can use the $ sign to represent jQuery, and you can get the value of an attribute of an HTML element (such as a <p> element) using the jQuery attr() function. For example, you can get the value of the id attribute of an HTML <p> element as follows:

```
var pId   = $("p").attr('id');
```

Additionally, you can get the text string in an HTML <p> element using the jQuery text() function, as shown here:

```
// get the text in the <p> element
var pText = $("p").text();
console.log (pId+' says '+pText);
```

Finally, you can update the text in an HTML <p> element using the jQuery text() function, as shown here:

```
// update the text in the <p> element
$("p").text("Goodbye World From a Paragraph");
```

Launch the file in Listing 10.1 and open the Web Inspector that is available in your WebKit-based browser. Next, select "Inspect Element," and click the ">>" symbol at the bottom of the Web page to see the output from the two console.log() statements in Listing 10.1.

You can use Chrome Web Inspector to view the contents of variables, which can be very helpful for debugging purposes. You can experiment with the features of Chrome Web Inspector, and also read online tutorials about this excellent tool.

QUERYING AND MODIFYING THE DOM WITH JQUERY

Earlier in this chapter, you saw how to use the jQuery eq() selector to find the first HTML <p> element in a set of <p> elements. This section shows you how to use various jQuery modifiers that make it very easy to find and update elements in an HTML5 Web page. The code samples are short because they illustrate only one or two qualifiers, but you can combine them to perform very sophisticated DOM traversals and context-sensitive modifications to DOM elements.

Some of the qualifiers that are discussed in the code samples in this section include :first, :last, :even, and :odd. A partial list of selectors includes :eq(), :lt(), :gt(), :has(), :contains(), and :eq().

Find and Modify Elements with :first and :last Qualifiers

The example in this section shows you how to use the jQuery :first and :last qualifiers to manipulate the text in HTML elements.

Listing 10.2 displays the contents of JQModifyElements1.html that illustrates how to switch the contents of two <p> elements.

LISTING 10.2: JQModifyElements1.html

```
<!DOCTYPE html>
<html lang="en">
<head>
  <meta charset="utf-8" />
  <title>jQuery and Modifying Elements</title>

  <script src="http://code.jquery.com/jquery-1.7.1.min.js">
  </script>
</head>

<body>
  <p style="color:red" id="Steve">Hello From Paragraph One</p>
  <p style="color:blue" id="Dave">Goodbye From Paragraph Two</p>

  <script>
   $(document).ready(function(){
     // get information in first paragraph:
     var pId1   = $("p:first").attr('id');
     var pText1 = $("p:first").text();

     // get information in last paragraph:
     var pId2   = $("p:last").attr('id');
     var pText2 = $("p:last").text();

     $("p:first").html(pText2);
```

```
      $("p:last").html(pText1);
     //$("p:first").text(pText2);
     //$("p:last").text(pText1);
     });
   </script>
  </body>
</html>
```

Listing 10.2 references the required jQuery file, adds two HTML <p> elements, and then extracts the value of the id attribute and the text in the first <p> element, as shown here:

```
// get information in first paragraph:
var pId1   = $("p:first").attr('id');
var pText1 = $("p:first").text();
```

The next block of code performs the same thing with the second <p> element, and then the text of the two <p> elements is switched with the following two lines of code:

```
$("p:first").html(pText2);
$("p:last").html(pText1);
```

Despite the simplicity of the jQuery code, this illustrates the ease with which you can manipulate HTML elements in an HTML Web page by means of the available jQuery functions.

Incidentally, you can get and set the value of an HTML <input> field (whose id attribute has value myInput) with the following two lines of code:

```
$("#myInput").val()
$("#myInput).text("new input value");
```

Figure 10.1 displays the result of rendering the page JQModifyElements1.htmlin a landscape-mode screenshot taken from an Asus Prime tablet with Android ICS.

The next section shows you how to use jQuery methods that can set collection of elements with the jQuery qualifiers :even() and :odd().

Finding Elements with :eq, :lt, and :gt Qualifiers

There are many jQuery functions available to perform sophisticated manipulations of HTML elements with relative ease. This section contains some useful code snippets that illustrate some of the other jQuery functions that are available.

For example, the jQuery qualifiers :eq(), :lt(), and :gt() match elements whose position is equal to, less than, or greater than, respectively, in a list of items. Recall that since lists in jQuery start from index 0, the first item in a list has index zero of the list.

An example of finding the <p> element with index 3:

```
$('p:eq(3)').text('index equals three');
```

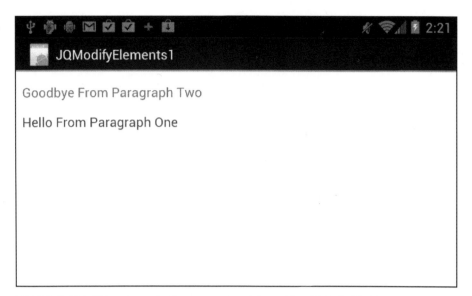

FIGURE 10.1 Modifying element in jQuery on an Asus Prime tablet with Android ICS

An example of finding the `<p>` element with an index greater than 3:

```
$('p:gt(3)').text('index is greater than three');
```

An example of finding the `<p>` element with an index less than 3:

```
$('p:lt(3)').text('index is less than three');
```

The preceding code snippets show you some of the things that are possible with jQuery functions.

There are jQuery functions that perform conditional tests on HTML elements. For example, jQuery provides custom selectors, such as `:has()`, `:contains()`, and `:eq()`. You can use these selectors to select elements, as in the following example:

```
$("div:contains('foo')"))
```

…and you can use these selectors to filter other selectors, as shown here:

```
$("div").contains('foo')
```

In addition, you can search for elements based on the value of their `id` attribute or by a specific `class` attribute, as shown in the next section.

Finding and Setting Element Attributes

You've seen how to use various jQuery functions to manipulate elements, and also how to find the value of an attribute. This section contains examples of updating the attributes of elements.

The following snippet gets the value of the `src` attribute of an element:

```
var $source = $("img").attr("src");
```

The next code snippet shows how to set the value of one attribute:

```
$("img").attr("src", "/images/MyHouse.jpg");
```

The following code snippet shows how to set multiple attributes in one command (displayed over multiple lines for convenience):

```
$("img").attr({
     src: "/images/MyHouse.jpg",
     title: "House",
     alt: "House"
});
```

Notice that the syntax of the jQuery `attr()` method is very similar to the jQuery `css()` method, so when you understand one function, you will understand the other one as well.

HTML5 supports custom attributes, provided that the attribute name starts with the string `data-` followed by an attribute name. Although you might not need to use custom attributes right now, jQuery Mobile relies heavily on custom attributes, so this functionality is extremely useful.

You can retrieve the values of custom attributes using the jQuery `.data()` method. For example, suppose your HTML Web page contains this snippet:

```
<div data-role="page" data-value="99" data-status="new"></div>
```

You can retrieve the values of these custom attributes as follows:

```
$("div").data("role") returns the value page
$("div").data("value") returns the value 99
$("div").data("status") returns the value true
```

You will see more examples of manipulating custom data attributes in jQuery Mobile code samples, and if you're really ambitious, you can find more examples in the jQuery Mobile source code.

Using jQuery to Remove Elements

As you can probably guess, jQuery enables you to remove elements in addition to finding and modifying elements in an HTML Web page. Listing 10.3 contains a portion of the HTML Web page `JQRemovingElements1.html` that illustrates how to remove elements via jQuery.

LISTING 10.3: JQRemovingElements1.html

```
<script>
  $(document).ready(function(){
    $("p:even").css({color:'white'});
    $("p:odd").css({color:'red'});
```

```
    $("p:first").css({color:'yellow'});
    $("p:last").css({color:'blue'});

    // remove the <p> element Dave
    $("#Dave").remove();

    // remove the <p> element Michelle
    $("div1").remove("#Michelle");

    // remove <p> elements containing "Goodbye"
    $("p").filter(":contains('Goodbye')").remove();
    });
  </script>
 </body>
</html>
```

Listing 10.3 contains three lines of code for removing elements, the first of which is shown here (the second is similar):

```
// remove the <p> element Dave
$("#Dave").remove();
```

Although the preceding code snippet performs just as you would expect, an example that illustrates the real power of jQuery is shown in the following code snippet, which uses the jQuery filter() method to find and then remove all the HTML <p> elements that contain the string Goodbye:

```
$("p").filter(":contains('Goodbye')").remove();
```

Compare the simple and intuitive nature of the preceding single line of jQuery code with the corresponding JavaScript code that is required to perform the same functionality.

Figure 10.2 displays the result of rendering RemovingElements1. html in a portrait-mode screenshot taken from an iOS application running on an iPad 3.

Creating DOM Elements

jQuery provides the clone() method and the append() method for creating new DOM elements. The clone() method creates a true copy of an element; if you specify true, then clone(true) will also propagate the event handlers of the source element. On the other hand, the append() method operates on the specified element. Listing 10.4 displays the contents of JQCreatingElements1.html that illustrates how to use both of these jQuery methods in order to create new elements in an HTML Web page.

LISTING 10.4: JQCreatingElements1.html

```
<!DOCTYPE html>
<html lang="en">
<body>
  <script>
```

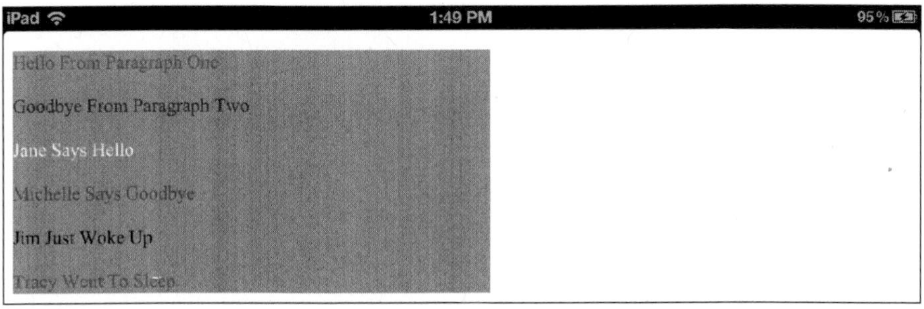

FIGURE 10.2 Removing elements jQuery on an iPad 3

```
$(document).ready(function(){
  // append a clone of the #Dave element to "#div2":
  $("#Dave").clone().css({color:"#000"}).appendTo("#div2");

  // append another clone of the #Dave element to "#div2":
  $("#Dave").clone().css({color:"#00f"}).appendTo("#div2");

  // move the red #Dave to the end of "#div4":
  $("#Dave").appendTo("#div4");

  // prepend #Dave to all the 'div' elements:
  //$("#Dave").clone().prependTo("div");
});
 </script>
 </body>
</html>
```

Listing 10.3 introduces the jQuery clone() method, an example of which is shown here:

```
// append a clone of the #Dave element to "#div2":
$("#Dave").clone().css({color:"#000"}).appendTo("#div2");
```

The purpose of the preceding code snippet is clear, and you can even read it from left to right to grasp its purpose: clone the element whose id is Dave, set its color to black, and append this cloned element to the element whose id is div2.

The only other new functionality in Listing 10.3 is the jQuery prepend-To() function, which inserts an element before (instead of after) a specified element, as shown here:

```
// prepend #Dave to all the 'div' elements:
//$("#Dave").clone().prependTo("div");
```

There are other jQuery methods for inserting DOM elements, some of which are described in the next section.

Figure 10.3 displays the result of rendering JQCreatingElements1. htmlin a landscape-mode screenshot taken from an iOS application running on an iPad 3.

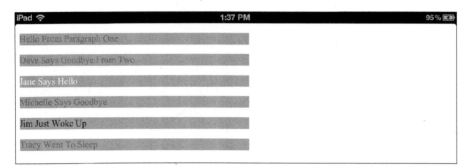

FIGURE 10.3 Creating elements with jQuery on an iPad 3

Useful jQuery Code Blocks

This section contains a set of code snippets that enable you to perform conditional logic and then execute your custom code. The code samples in this section are straightforward, and the comments explain their purpose.

Check if jQuery is loaded:
```
if (typeof jQuery == 'undefined') {
   // jQuery is not loaded
}
```

Check if an element exists:
```
if ( $('#myElement').length > 0 ) {
   // the element exists
}
```

Check for empty elements:
```
$('*').each(function() {
   if ($(this).text() == "") {
      //do something here
   }
});
```

Returns true or false based on content of a <div> element:
```
var emptyTest = $('#myDiv').is(':empty');
```

Determine if a checkbox is checked (returns true/false):
```
$('#checkBox').attr('checked');
```

Find all checked checkboxes:
```
$('input[type=checkbox]:checked');
```

Disable/enable inputs for a button element:
```
$("#submit-button").attr("disabled", true);
```

Remove an attribute from a button element:
```
$("#submit-button").removeAttr("disabled");
```

Another important class of jQuery functions involves functions that enable you to navigate around the DOM, and some of these methods are discussed in the next section.

HANDLING CLICK EVENTS IN JQUERY

jQuery provides support for various types of events and user gestures that you can "bind" to custom code (written by you) that is executed whenever those events or gestures take place. The events that you can detect and bind in jQuery Mobile include `click`, `tap`, `taphold`, `swipe`, `swipeleft`, and `swiperight`.

The `click()` function enables you to handle click events, and one example of the syntax is here:

```
$("#button1").click(function() {
    // do something
}
```

There are several techniques for handling events, and the recommended technique for doing so is shown here:

```
$("#button1").on("click"), function() {
    // do something
}
```

In a similar fashion, you can use the two preceding code snippets to define event handlers for the other jQuery events shown above as well as the mouse events that are listed in an upcoming section.

The `dblclick()` function enables you to handle double click events. An example of the syntax is here:

```
$("#button2").dblclick(function() {
    // do something
}
```

The `focus()` function provides focus on selected elements. For example, this code displays a cursor when you click on an input field whose `id` attribute equals `firstInput`:

```
$("#firstInput").focus(function() {
    // do something
});
```

Listing 10.5 displays most of the contents of `JQClickDivs1.html` that illustrates how to detect click events and then update the contents of both `<div>` elements in this HTML5 Web page.

LISTING 10.5: JQClickDivs1.html

```
<!DOCTYPE html>
```

```
<html lang="en">
<head>
  <meta charset="utf-8" />
  <title>Detecting Click Events with jQuery</title>
  <script src="jquery-1.7.1.js"></script>
</head>

<body>
  <div id="div1">The first div element </div>
  <div id="div2">The second div element </div>

  <script>
  var click1=0, click2=0, total=0;

  $(document).ready(function() {
     $("#div1").click(function() {
        ++click1;
        ++total;
        $(this).text("Clicked: "+click1+" total: "+total);
        $("#div2").text("Clicked: "+click2+" total: "+total);
     });

     $("#div2").click(function() {
        ++click2;
        ++total;
        $(this).text("Clicked: "+click2+" total: "+total);
        $("#div1").text("Clicked: "+click1+" total: "+total);
     });
  });
  </script>
</body>
</html>
```

Listing 10.5 references the required jQuery file, followed by some CSS styling definitions, along with two HTML <div> elements. The code for adding a click event listener to the first HTML <div> element is shown here (with similar jQuery code for the second HTML <div> element):

```
$("#div1").click(function() {
    ++click1;
    ++total;
    $(this).text("Clicked: "+click1+" total: "+total);
    $("#div2").text("Clicked: "+click2+" total: "+total);
});
```

Whenever users click on the preceding HTML <div> element, its click count and the total click count are incremented, and the text of both HTML <div> elements are updated with the click count for the individual <div> elements as well as the sum of the click counts for both <div> elements.

Although the example in Listing 10.4 is simplistic, it does illustrate how to keep track of events in different HTML elements in an HTML Web page. A more realistic example could involve an HTML Web page with an HTML Form that has inter-dependencies between elements in the form.

Figure 10.4 displays the result of rendering the HTML page `JQClickDivs1.html` in a landscape-mode screenshot taken from an Android application running on an Asus Prime tablet with Android ICS.

FIGURE 10.4 Counting click events on an Asus Prime tablet with Android ICS

CHAINING JQUERY FUNCTIONS

You have already seen examples of chaining jQuery commands, and this section shows you how to execute more sophisticated chained commands. Specifically, the code sample in this section shows you how to use the `.end()` method, which enables you to "reset" the context list whenever you need to do so in a sequence of chained commands.

By comparison, you might have used chained commands in Java (especially with JAXB) such as the following:

```
myList().getFirstElem().getCustomer().setFirstName("Dave");
```

However, jQuery chaining can involve more sophisticated operations because you can change the reference to the current result set before applying a new operation.

ACCELEROMETER VALUES WITH JQUERY

The example in this section illustrates how you can use jQuery to obtain accelerometer values for a mobile device.

Listing 10.6 displays the contents of `JQAccelerometer1.html` that illustrates how to display the accelerometer values of a mobile device whenever the device undergoes acceleration in any direction. The CSS stylesheet `JQAccelerometer1.css` contains simple selectors that are not shown here, but you can find the complete listing on the DVD.

LISTING 10.6: JQAccelerometer1.html

```
<!DOCTYPE html>
<html lang="en">
<head>
 <meta charset="utf-8" />
 <title>jQuery and Accelerometer</title>
 <script
     src="http://ajax.googleapis.com/ajax/libs/jquery/1.6.4/jquery.
min.js">
 </script>

<script>
    var colorX = "", colorY = "", colorZ = "";
    var intx = 0, inty = 0, intz = 0;
    var colors = ['#f00', '#ff0', '#00f'];

    $('document').ready(function(){
      $(window).bind("devicemotion", function(e){
        var accelEvent = e.originalEvent,
            acceler = accelEvent.accelerationIncludingGravity,
            x = acceler.x, y = acceler.y, z = acceler.z;
        if(x < 0)      { intx = 0; }
        else if(x < 1) { intx = 1; }
        else           { intx = 2; }
```

```
            if (y < 0)       { inty = 0; }
            else if (y < 1)  { inty = 1; }
            else             { inty = 2; }

            if (z < 0)       { intz = 0; }
            else if (z < 1)  { intz = 1; }
            else             { intz = 2; }

            colorX = colors[intx];
            colorY = colors[inty];
            colorZ = colors[intz];

            $("#valueX").css("backgroundColor", colorX);
            $("#valueY").css("backgroundColor", colorY);
            $("#valueZ").css("backgroundColor", colorZ);

               $("#valueX").html("<p>Acceleration x: <b>" + x + "</b></
p>");
               $("#valueY").html("<p>Acceleration y: <b>" + x + "</b></
p>");
               $("#valueZ").html("<p>Acceleration z: <b>" + x + "</b></
p>");
          });
       });
    </script>
</head>

<body>
    <h2>Accelerometer Values</h2>
    <div id="outer">
      <div id="valueX"></div>
      <div id="valueY"></div>
      <div id="valueZ"></div>
    </div>
  </body>
</html>
```

The code in Listing 10.6 obtains accelerometer values for three directions (all perpendicular to each other) for a mobile device, and then performs some arithmetic in order to compute integer values to be used as indexes in an array of color values. After determining the color associated with each direction, the associated rectangular `<div>` element is updated with the corresponding color.

After binding the `window` object to the `devicemotion` event, we can use the event object (in this case it's called `e`) to obtain a JavaScript reference to the acceleration object (which is called `acceler`) and then extract current values for the three different axes, as shown here:

```
$('document').ready(function(){
    $(window).bind("devicemotion", function(e){
      var accelEvent = e.originalEvent,
            acceler = accelEvent.accelerationIncludingGravity,
            x = acceler.x, y = acceler.y, z = acceler.z;
```

For simplicity, the array contains only three colors, and the following code computes a number between 0 and 2 in order to determine the color for the x direction:

```
if(x < 0)      { intx = 0; }
else if(x < 1) { intx = 1; }
else           { intx = 2; }
```

The color for the x direction is calculated like this:

```
colorX = colors[intx];
```

The background color of the HTML `<div>` element that is associated with the x direction is updated with the following code:

```
$("#valueX").css("backgroundColor", colorX);
```

Finally, the current value of the acceleration in the x direction is displayed using the following code snippet:

```
$("#valueX").html("<p>Acceleration x: <b>" + x + "</b></p>");
```

The corresponding values for the y direction and the z direction are computed in a similar fashion.

Figure 10.5 displays the result of rendering the HTML web page in Listing 10.5 in a landscape-mode screenshot taken from an Android application running on an Asus Prime tablet with Android ICS.

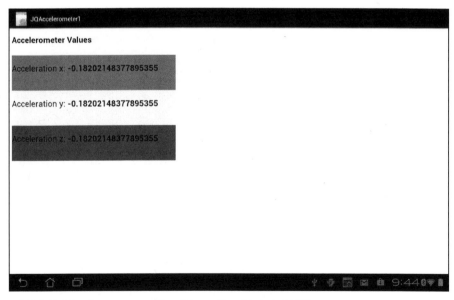

FIGURE 10.5 Accelerometer on an Asus Prime tablet with Android ICS

SUMMARY

This chapter introduced you to jQuery, along with code samples that illustrated how to use jQuery functions to create simple animation effects. You saw code samples that showed how to do the following:

- Create a simple jQuery-based HTML5 Web page
- Find and modify elements with :first and :last qualifiers
- Find elements with :even and :odd qualifiers
- Find elements with :eq, :lt, and :gt qualifiers
- Find elements by class or id
- Find/set element attributes
- Find form elements and their attributes
- CSS3-style expressions for finding elements
- Remove DOM elements
- Create DOM elements
- Handle events in jQuery
- Use the click() function
- Chaining jQuery functions
- Accelerometer with jQuery

ON THE DVD

Please refer to the companion disc to view Appendix A and Appendix B:

Appendix A: jQuery Concepts

Appendix B: Introduction to Android

INDEX